A JOURNAL OF AWAKENING
AND DELIVERANCE

SATYAM NADEEN

NEW F★R★E★E★DOM PRESS

ISBN 0-9653850-0-0
First Printing
August 1996

Cover
Photograph
Jill Fineberg

Illustrations
Ashisha

Layout, Design,
Lettering
Joy Franklin

Typesetting
Karen A. Sanderson

Text set in Palatino.

2nd printing - August, 1997

Satyam Nadeen's Web Site: http://wolfcrk.com/nadeen

NEW F★R★E★E★DOM PRESS
P.O. Box 3029
San Rafael, CA 94912
1-888-363-3738

Consciousness is all there is.
You are not the doer,
and neither is anyone else.

CONTENTS

PART 3

LIFE IN THE FOURTH DIMENSION

INTRODUCTION

This little journal is a personal story about a journey of awakening. A true story. A story with a comic ending. It doesn't turn out the way you would expect a story about awakening to end. That's why it's funny. It is tied into the cosmic joke of the human predicament. The bottom line of this story is not to encourage you to seek awakening. If you think you are going to get some do's and don'ts about a path to or from awakening, you are out of luck already. In fact, the whole point of this tale is to assure you it is perfectly divine to forget all about awakening and just embrace yourself and those around you as absolutely right on course just the way you and they are.

So then, this being so, why would I even want to write a comic book about a no-path, no-goal, wake-up call? I am clear that all the information here is totally available from your own inner voice of wisdom. I am equally clear that many may not understand these strange conclusions or even agree with them. But because the times they are a-shifting, I have already witnessed the changes in me inspiring like changes in those with whom I am sharing this new information and experience. What's the point? Well, I have been away to a maximum security prison for the last several years. Away from my family, friends, playmates, and loved ones. Now the prison gates are about to swing open, and everyone naturally wants to know how life was behind the big wall all this time. Rather than launch into multiple, lengthy explanations, I just wrote out this little story, sort of like a welcome-home letter to all my friends out there, whether we have met yet or not.

READER ADVISORY WARNING!

This is to advise you that there are some very dangerous curves ahead that may cause you to spin out of control. The reason for this is that everything you read in the way of new material tends to enter your intellect through the left side of the brain, which is the analytical, logical, normal reasoning function of the left hemisphere. However, this journey is designed to bypass this process of logic and enter your being directly through the right hemisphere, which is the intuitive, creative side of functioning. What I am about to relate to you, you already know at some deep, subconscious, intuitive, sort of *déjà vu* level. But your logical mind is going to scream out in protest because it won't fit your normal preconditioned model of how you experience life in the third dimension. Especially when we get to the juicy parts, like free will for example.

So this is to advise you of a suggested way to switch channels here, and maybe receive the material through the right side of the brain. First of all, don't read too much at one time. A chapter or two a day is more than enough of this material to digest with a modicum of comprehension. Second, don't even think about or try to figure out the material in your mind after you read it. It doesn't fit in the left side of the brain, so forget it! Normally, this material is not comprehended by reason alone. But it will be operating in subtle areas that are only receptive to your deepest knowing levels, and that is your intuitive core essence. Third, read this story with an open mind. Just relax into a mental space where you suspend all the normal logic that you have acquired from birth on through various conditionings. Embrace the possibility that this fourth dimensional perspective may just possibly be a light of truth you may like to hear.

You don't have to arrive at any conclusions when you finish the book. Instead of having to understand this material and embrace it as your own, just understand it enough that you could explain it to friends if they asked you about it, not that you agree with any of it. This allows time for an initial intellectual comprehension of the words to percolate down into the heart and one day explode into your personal knowing at a gut level.

If you heed this advice, strange sensations may begin to appear farther down the road. Because your essence has been exposed to something that it already knows at its core level, and because you didn't resist any of it with your logical mind, even though it doesn't meet with your remembered model of experience, it is now at work within you like a delightful private investigator who operates under cover. You may begin to shift your whole perspective until you end up in a new fourth dimensional way of reacting to the human predicament. Once you start heaving deep sighs of recognition later on, as it bonds with your new daily encounters with Spirit, feel free to start discussing these concepts with yourself or your loved ones. Until then, intuition and creativity in Spirit work best in quiet, nonthinking, alone time.

I think it can safely be said that if you feel you are a sincere, open seeker of your true Self, and you can now empty out your cup of *all* previous knowledge, both spiritual and metaphysical, scriptural and religious, then this tale will plant and water a seed of freedom that will explode with a new vision some time soon. And just as safe to say, if you have any investment in maintaining your present status quo, for whatever reasons, you will experience too much resistance from all your previous layers of conditioning in the human predicament to break free right now.

So consider yourselves advised. This is a dangerous story for those who are uncomfortable with mental nudity.

PART 1

THE WAKE-UP CALL

CHAPTER 1

THE
LOTTERY
PAYOFF

Have you ever wondered what it would be like to win one of those 100 million dollar state lotteries that are ever present these days? Winning one would surely gain you freedom in at least one area—financial. But then it couldn't really fulfill all your other needs: health, satisfying love in relationships, freedom from violence, boredom, loneliness, etc. But now, imagine with me, a universal lottery happening where all of your needs were supplied now and for all eternity. The odds on winning a state lottery of a 100 million dollars are around one in 200 million. So the odds of winning a universal lottery would have to be at least one in the billions. Just one fortunate human being a year to benefit so much—just think of it! Yet the story I'm about to share with you is precisely about a similar situation to experience, by pure chance alone, that universal payoff, and the very fact that you are reading this book is your very own lottery ticket. However, in this lottery, we have many millions of winners every year, so your odds are even more favorable.

The big payoff I am referring to is a state of total enlightenment, where your true nature as the Godhead shines through in a known, felt, and fully lived experience. Winning total enlightenment is not a problem at all though, because EVERYONE, by the very fact of being alive and conscious, is already precisely that—PURE ENLIGHTENMENT. In fact, the only obstacle to feeling your own enlightenment is your not knowing that you are already totally enlightened! So for the rest of this story, I'm not going to even talk about the term "enlightenment" so much as I am about your wake-up call or "awakening" to who you really are.

I love the idea of the big universal lottery, because for the past year I've walked around feeling so overwhelmed with gratitude that winning such a lottery would actually pale by comparison to what is going on right now after my wake-up call and the deliverance and rapture that accompany it.

This story is reaching out to touch all of you who have considered yourselves "seekers" for awakening and are still waiting to be "finders." Just in case you have been snake-bit with the venom of seeking, maybe I can share some of the antidote for the finding. My own seeking went on for half a century until one day, quite gratuitously, it just happened. Not because of me, but quite in spite of me. Perhaps in sharing this journey with you, it will assuage the thirst you suffer from with a cool drink of one man's reality. Not any reality you may have heard of so far on your journey, but slightly different. One that is so simple and direct that we have all overlooked it throughout all our seeking, even though it was quite by Divine design. And the big surprise comes from the fact that all it takes for you to wake up is possibly to hear a simple truth intuitively, with your whole being, that I will share with you later on. When I heard it, I woke up. When the awakened one who relayed it to me through his book heard it from his teacher, he woke up. And the teacher before him, and so on.

When I finally share this masterpiece of simplicity with you, either you will feel Grace and Destiny waiting for you in this moment, with goose bumps of intuitive knowing, or you just might say: "You mean that's all there is to it? Hey, forget it, 'cause it's no big deal!" But then you will also continue on as a merry seeker instead of relaxing into the new role of finder.

Now I know that I am going way out on a limb by announcing that I've had a wake-up call and that it is definitely available without effort, without spiritual disciplines, and is in the fine tradition of American fast foods—available right now!

You wouldn't have been drawn to even read this book if

your head wasn't already in the mouth of the tiger, so there is no escaping your awakening now. Don't start dancing on the ceiling just yet. Keep in mind that while your awakening may be sudden, the ramifications of it, or what I like to call "the deliverance," are not so sudden. In fact, I would venture to say that the deliverance will most likely continue for many, many years afterward.

That is why the title *From Onions to Pearls* was chosen. What we all are is a pure Pearl of Consciousness, God-essence, if you like, without anything possible to be added on for self-realization. But by Divine design, this Pearl, from the moment of birth onward, has been surrounded by layer after layer of conditioning. So what "awakening" consists of is the realization that you are indeed this perfect Pearl of Consciousness; and then the "deliverance" takes over by removing each subtle layer of conditioning until only the Pearl again remains.

CHAPTER 2

PERSONAL BACKGROUND

I was born into a large Irish family, the eldest of several children. By second grade I was already "seeking" by yearning to become a Catholic priest. I entered the seminary when I was 12 years old and continued my studies in high school, majoring in philosophy as an undergraduate and theology in graduate school at the Catholic University of America in Washington, D.C. When I finally saw the light and left, I was already 26 years old. My direction then shifted as I also left Catholicism and pursued Eastern tradition through the usual approach of hatha yoga,[1] meditation, and Zen practice. Consider me your typical inspired "New Ager" for the next 30 years. I guru-hopped from Maharishi Mahesh Yogi to Guru Maharaji and spent years with Shri Bhagwan Rajneesh, later known as Osho. You name the latest fad in workshops and there I was, plugged in. Esalen in Big Sur and Rajneeshpuram in Oregon became my second homes. To concisely sum it all up, I had been in

> therapy, and was
> rolfed
> ESTed
> rebirthed.

I discovered my inner child
> my wild man within
> my feminine side of masculinity.

All the while, I consulted
> workshops
> seminars
> encounter groups

> meditation circles
> retreats
> psychics
> tea leaves
> Ouija boards
> astrologers
> channelers
> numerologists
> aura readers
> palm readers
> tarot cards.

As I plugged into

> macrobiotic diets
> colonics
> liver cleanses
> chanting mantras
> wearing malas
> cracking koans
> weight training
> aerobics
> vegetarianism
> fruitarianism
> 40-day water fasts.

And just to keep perspective, I had my chakras balanced. Does any of this sound familiar, fellow seekers?

In addition to all the usual spiritual and psychotherapeutic disciplines, I experimented with all the psychedelics and psychotropics available in my search to expand my horizons. One in particular, MDMA, or ecstasy, became for me in 1979 a *tour de force* and I embarked on a self-imposed mission to save the world through this miracle mood enhancer. In 1988 this substance was declared illegal by the Drug Enforcement Agency for the United States. Not to be deterred by a technicality, I moved my whole operation out of the United States to other countries where it was still legal. But life being full of change and surprises, a small quantity of the drug slipped through the cracks back into the United States, and I was subsequently arrested and convicted on a conspiracy charge, then sentenced to seven and a half years in federal prison. Now this is where it got intriguing!

For the first two years after my arrest, I was held in a small county jail in Florida while awaiting sentencing. This was a dungeonlike structure with no windows, no air conditioning, no ventilation. (The vents were there but the motors were always broken.) There was no exercise or movement allowed. The average temperature combined with the high humidity was a year-round average of well over 100 degrees. Previously, my body fat was always a lean 10 percent, but during this period of Southern-style, greasy fried foods, it ballooned up over 30 percent. We were kept like feedlot cattle in pens built for 10 men, but they stuffed 32 of us in each holding cell, with recent arrivals all sleeping on the floor. There was one open toilet for all of us. Now add to this the shock of finding myself the only white boy in a cell full of young, violent, black gang-bangers who have a bit of an attitude about how blacks have been abused for the last 200 years. These youngsters all had their own boom box radios. Each one was tuned to a different rap station played 24/7 [2] at full volume. This ended up being a hell more wild than Dante's *Inferno* or St. John's dark night of the soul.

Here I was, 54 years old, having led a quiet, cultured, gentle, and for the last 28 years, luxurious life, now thrown into a subculture of survival of the fittest. There was at least one gang rape, suicide, and murder attempt per week the whole two years I was there, some of them successful. On top of everything else, I was having to face up to the fact that the DEA had taken every possession I owned in four countries and was also trying to put my ex-wife Pauline away and place our daughter in an orphanage. They had promised me life in prison without parole if they had their way about it. Don't think that the idea of suicide as a quick way out didn't pass through my mind. If there had been a nice, clean pill as an alternative to a messy self-inflicted death, it may have been more appealing.

While this part may sound a bit bleak, and it was a bummer, there was a balance point to it. Such absolute and total suppression of life as I had known it served to completely annihilate the old identity of "self." Here I was desperately trying to hang onto my sanity and physical life, and all my old self-images of who I thought I was, were being wiped out in this dark night of the soul. This time period helped to soften up what little was left of the ego so that the process of listening to the voice of inner wisdom could come through. And this brings us to the awakening phase.

---

[1] Hatha Yoga: The system of practicing the movement of various asanas, or postures, that help the union of the individual with God.

[2] 24/7: Prison term for 24 hours a day/7 days a week.

THE PROCESS OF AWAKENING

While the process of awakening itself feels very sudden and dramatic, the events leading up to it are probably gradual. Sometimes tragic events like life threatening illnesses, loss of mobility, a career, a loved one, or financial setbacks, etc., help to soften up the tough exterior of all our layers of identity so that the inner wisdom of who we really are can emerge.

In reading about the awakening experience of others who have described their process, I have found some common denominators.

There is a deathlike experience involving loss of ego or personal identity.

There is a letting go of trying to understand the whole process or anything else relating to God or spiritual matters.

Finally, there is a letting go of all intentional effort toward awakening.

Initially this is followed by waves of bliss that later simmer down to a feeling of deep peace.

Those two years spent in that "black hole of Calcutta" that was called a county jail awaiting sentencing, were the last intense "seeking" of my journey. I had access to any and all books, tapes, and videos that were sent to me, and since I could not leave my metal bunk, I just lay there and overdosed on metaphysical and meditational input. Just as I was leaving that county jail to be transferred to a federal prison at Terminal Island in San Pedro, California, the first shock waves of intuitive knowing hit me. They centered around a practice of self-inquiry

I had been doing very intensively: "Who Am I?" It dawned on me that I couldn't know anything about God or the spiritual path with this limited mind, so I just gave it up. With this surrender came the first tidal wave of relief and bliss. A few weeks later I was in Terminal Island adjusting to seeing for the first time in two years the sun, moon, stars, ocean, sea gulls, pelicans, seals, flowers, trees, and grass when I was hit by the second phase of this surrender process. Not only didn't I know anything about enlightenment, I couldn't do anything about it either! Once again this was followed by tsunami-sized waves of bliss and relief. The awakening itself was now complete. What followed were the ramifications of this intuitive knowing in my daily life. This process I have come to call "the deliverance."

But let's stay with this awakening process a while longer here. To prepare this individual bag of skin for awakening, Spirit had no qualms about ruthlessly crushing any notion of a personal identity or "ego," the "me" part which it had so carefully prepared and nurtured up to this point.

Not only was I jerked out of a comfortable life of fun and loving support and then stuck into that "black hole of Calcutta," but I suffered a psychic death that was every bit as real as the final curtain call. From the day of my arrest and for at least two months thereafter, I felt like a walking, talking, dead person with no idea of who I was, only that there was no longer any connection to that which I had formerly considered "me." But somehow I knew that however terrifying this death experience was, it was connected to a rebirth soon to come. What I liked even better was the idea that I would be reborn into a 50-something-year-old body instead of having to suffer the indignities of infancy again.

Okay, I own up to having inspired times in the years before (probably under the influence of magic mushrooms) when I cried out, "Lord, take me now at any cost. I want to go home! I'll do anything to reach you." However, I don't believe the final death of the ego is ever painless or ever voluntarily let go of, no matter what your ignorant mouth is saying.

However strange it seemed to me at the time, about a year into the county jail scene, suddenly out of nowhere I was struck with an interest in reading the works of Ramana Maharshi, a name out of the distant past, one mentioned by Rajneesh. For the preceding year I had been listening to several hundred tapes by channeled entities like Ramtha, Seth, Abraham, Lazarus, Emanuel, Bartholomew (my favorite), and countless "ascension" masters, like Sananda and Ashtar. So you see, for me to request Ramana was a request out of left field at the time. Along with Ramana's books, my friend included a copy of *I Am That* by Maharaj Nasargadatta, and *Wake Up and Roar*, I and II by Poonjaji. Basically, all these men are from the spiritual tradition of advaita vedanta,[1] or nondualism, and maintain a fairly straight line of reasoning along these lines. It was certainly interesting. I enjoyed their works at the time and read them over and over again, because there was something there beckoning to me. But it was one Ramesh Balsekar, a student disciple of Nasargadatta, whose book I again coincidentally found a year later after reading the other advaita guys, that really did me in. Now he's not saying anything different from his buddies, but he said it, delivered with Grace, in just one sentence that hit me right in the intuitive heart. His masters had given me some advaita tidbits that took a year to percolate down to my heart, along with many mantras like the "Who am I?" kind of inquiries and *voila!* Lightning struck home. All he said in his opening chapter was "Consciousness (Source—All That Is—God) is all there is." WOW!!! He said it and I could actually see it, know it, feel on fire with it, and begin to live it.

In the advaita school, God is the Source and the Subject of all Consciousness. Everything else is the appearance or object of the Subject as phenomena. But in this case, Subject and object are one and the same energy.

The role of a "doer" can only pertain to the Subject once we conceptually separate these two words of Subject and object in the world of duality or appearance.

The role of the one "done," or puppet if you like, can only

be the object of the subject, and not the subject of further objects.

> The bottom line, folks! You have no free will.
> You don't make the choices.
> You are not the doer.
> Neither is anyone else out there the doer.

There is only Consciousness acting through the individual mind/body organism that we call this bag of skin and bones.

Once you get this, and I mean really get it, say, like St. Paul got it when he was struck down by some kind of Divine Lightning and in a flash clearly saw the ignorance of his former thinking, then I would say you have received your wake-up call. The very thought that Consciousness is all there is, and I am not the doer, kept me in a blissful swoon for months. It's easy to understand how Buddha just sat there for a couple of weeks under the Bodhi tree when he got his wake-up call. Ramana Maharshi sat on a mountaintop for three years without moving when his alarm clock went off. In fact, his body was so emaciated and eaten up by insects he almost didn't make it off that mountain.

The awakening itself is a sudden event. It may seem like the events leading up to it are a gradual happening, but here's what happens. Let's say we are all climbing steps toward awakening. Destiny, the handmaiden of Source, dictates that on the 697th step, so and so will be awakened. So he plows along for years and years and reaches step #692, where he starts to see the light shining over the horizon. But when step #697 is reached, POW! There it is, seemingly sudden, even though it took 696 prior steps to soften him up before he reached it.

So there, now you have been given the magic alarm clock for your wake-up call:

> "Consciousness is all there is."
> "You are not the doer."

So why didn't I respond to this penetrating concept the whole time I was reading Ramana, Nasargadatta, and Poonjaji the preceding year? They all said it, more or less, though not in those exact words? Because I hadn't reached my preordained step yet. But when I "accidentally" came across a book by Ramesh and read his opening statement, there I was, just leaving my symbolic step #696 with one foot poised in midair. My whole preceding 54 years had been a softening process for this one awesome moment. The whole two years in that county jail cell had sufficiently removed any clinging to a "me" identity so that Source could now penetrate and permeate as the identity of Subject I AM THAT.

[1] Advaita vedanta: Nondualism. The doctrine that contends only the Source—the Absolute—the Ultimate Principle has existence, and that all phenomenal existence is illusion.

CHAPTER 4

THE DELIVERANCE

I had always believed, by virtue of my multilayered conditioning, that once you were "awakened," basically that was the end of the whole process. But experience quickly taught me that was just the beginning, that "awakening" was only the first step of the process of "deliverance." Once the full impact of "Consciousness is all there is" and "I am not the doer" hits you, you realize who you really are and are not. From this profound realization flows the ramifications of this new "Pearl Vision" that will permeate every detail of your daily life.

These ramifications have applied to all aspects of life and it is that which I call the "deliverance." Remember the original idea at the beginning of the book in which I discussed how we have covered up this pure Pearl of Consciousness with onion-like layers of conditioning. When you view the world of appearance through the distortion of this conditioning, I call that "onion vision." However, when the awakening happens, there is a total and complete switchover to viewing life now from the Pearl of Consciousness that you really are. You view from the advantage of Source and not from what you have been conditioned as an onion to believe from birth. But please understand that, while you now have "Pearl Vision," you still have a lifetime of conditioned layers that need to be removed. That part is not a sudden or momentary happening. Maybe a few of the "biggies" like Jesus or Krishna had a sudden and spontaneous deliverance, but that seems to be an exception to the natural process that may well take the rest of your life.

In my own case, what would occur goes something like

this: I'm walking along, swept away in the awesome rapture of knowing and feeling "I Am That," when a hostile guard or racially bigoted inmate gang-banger picks me out to be harassed. At first—fear, followed possibly by anger, and the inevitable "Why me, Lord?" This all happens in the first few seconds of conditioned response. But then I hear this clear inner voice of deliverance saying something like "All here is not what it seems! That threatening person is not your enemy. That is an appearance of Consciousness just as you are. And as you are not able to make choices on how you act, neither is he. This whole scenario you are engaged in and witnessing is part of the Leela,[1] or "Divine play of Source amusing Itself." When that kind of scene repeats itself enough times, finally that particular layer of viewing someone as a potential enemy who threatens you is removed for good. The initial conditioned reflex of "onion vision" is almost instantly replaced by "Pearl Vision," and as the deliverance continues and the understanding deepens, the rapture is prolonged and intensified. Even when you finally think you have been delivered from all the layers of "onion vision," there is always one more that unique circumstances will happen to bring up for review. You will be amazed at the almost infinite number of finite concepts we have in our inherited conventional wisdom that are gradually weeded out by the wisdom of "Pearl Vision." We will touch on some of these before the story ends.

[1] Leela: Play, sport. The divine play of the Source.

CHAPTER 5

THE
RAPTURE

Do you remember when you were still a virgin and your friends discussed having an orgasm? You could only imagine what they might be referring to. But once you experienced your first orgasm, there was no doubt in your mind whether or not you had actually experienced it. There's too much difference between having and not having one to doubt it. Well, the same knowing applies to the "awakening." Along with the "deliverance" of awakening comes the "rapture." But unlike an orgasm that lasts only a few seconds, the rapture basically is happening almost all of the time. Once you know—"I AM THAT"—you are never the same again.

I can't give you an accurate definition of the rapture, but I can describe it. The first and predominant experience of the rapture is the overwhelming sense of freedom. For me this was ironic, because I always heard that bliss was the main ingredient of awakening, and here I was in a maximum security prison with gun towers and razor wire fences surrounding me, and all I could feel was freedom. Yes, there is some bliss too, but it's not as predominant or as constant as the experience of total freedom from limitation. When bliss hits you, you are a dysfunctional ninny while it's in motion, whereas the pervading sense of freedom allows you to carry on with normal life.

The secondary effect of the rapture is a deep, deep sense of profound peace. The peace that the Bible talks about that surpasses all understanding. Part of this peace comes from the knowing that since Consciousness is all there is, then all is truly well and good. It's like you are in the free fall of life and the human predicament, but you have this immense safety net that will catch you should fear arise. Where I used to live in a sea of suffering and inner conflict, with an occasional island of relief, the rapture now allows me to live in a sea of peace, with an occasional island of momentary contraction. Before awakening, no matter how much wealth, health, romantic love, power, or adult toys I possessed, there was always a constant free-floating, high anxiety that something was terribly wrong, that some catastrophe was surely imminent, and that I had landed on the wrong planet by some accident of birth. Right below the surface of feeling imminent doom was another gadfly provoking high anxiety. Somehow I needed to do something terribly important, but I just didn't know what it was. And so there ensued a constant battle, using my weapons of distraction like drugs, sex, and rock and roll to momentarily ease the discomfort or outright suffering caused by living with these anxieties.

Rapture changed all that into a constant knowing that not only is all well, but also there is nowhere to go, nothing to do, and understanding is everything. Another level of rapture is the sweet delight of experiencing everything through the eyes of Source, as fresh and new. All of nature, all other humans, everything animate and inanimate is equal and pure Consciousness, to be embraced and appreciated as such. What is—as is! What a delight! And since you are no longer responsible for any causality or effects, the rapture allows you to enjoy whatever is—as it is! No need to change, improve, ameliorate, or eliminate anything. Just be, and enjoy what is—as is! The experience is akin to a constant hum or buzz of joy. It's not the dysfunctional bliss that blows you away occasionally, when all you can do is weep with sobs of gratitude.

To tell you the truth, I would have expected compassion to be the predominant expression of awakening and the rapture. After all, I had read a lot of material about Buddha and his heavy emphasis on compassion. But somehow seeing the world and the human predicament from the viewpoint of

Source, all that I see is what is – as is, exactly as it is supposed to be—fully animated, designed and running on the inner wisdom of Consciousness. So, my reaction is: "Ah, life is gooooood!" I see through the apparent suffering now as a balanced equation of freedom and limitation in which Consciousness is amusing Itself. In Genesis after creating the world, God is reputed to have said: "All my creation is good." This has become my definition of love. Embracing what is – as is, because Consciousness is all there is. Yes, there is still sensitivity and empathy to the suffering of others, but all is not as it seems. Deliverance then becomes a vehicle to deepen the understanding that connects the human predicament of suffering to the embrace of it as the unfathomable Wisdom of Source.

From the first moments of awakening, the rapture provided a brand new experience. Let's call this sensation "original innocence regained." You have all heard of "original sin." To me this is the state of being designed by Source to create the human predicament. Part of our physical makeup includes a brain or intellect, whose function as a receiver of Consciousness is to go through sensory data, instantly analyze it, compare it and come up with judgments that fall within the polarities like: Good or bad, acceptable or unacceptable, and like or dislike. This is by Divine design, although any judgment results in a contraction of limitation. Even if you judge something as wonderful, the concept of "wonderful" is not available unless its counterpart "horrible" is also somehow present. Adam and Eve lost their original innocence and got thrown out of the Garden of Eden when they ate from the tree of knowledge of good and evil. In other words, they went from their pristine state of bliss in original innocence to the conflict of original sin by having to judge every thought from then on. Now the process has been reversed again, and in seeing through the eyes of Source, accepting everything as an extension of Consciousness and what is – as is, judgments, comparisons, and opinions are no longer relevant. And you feel as though an enormous weight has been lifted off of your head and soul. This is what I call my original innocence regained, and it is an integral part of the rapture. This is what I define as freedom.

CHAPTER 6

THE NATURE OF CONSCIOUSNESS

When I described the first phase of awakening, for me it was a death to everything meaningful that I knew in life up to that point. Then followed a surrender to ever figuring out how Spirit works. So all efforts, like reading or listening to metaphysical tapes, ceased. I was content in my not knowing because the burden of finding out the mysteries of the universe had been lifted. It wasn't until about a year into the deliverance that the nature of how Consciousness functions began to manifest itself more clearly in my understanding.

I used to wonder why a God of omniscience, omnipotence, and omnipresence, in other words, unlimited in every way, would want to create a universe where evil, suffering, and pain were rampant. Of course, I had in the back of my mind, through conditioning, the concept of a personal God. The masters of advaita can help us out here with their theory of understanding. They view God in an impersonal sense—no great white-bearded father image is possible in the understanding of Consciousness being all there is. So they say that Consciousness as the Source in an unmanifested state is "Satchitananda."[1] (Sat = eternal reality, chit = pure awareness, ananda = bliss.) Source is completely aware and blissful, but in this state of rest, It cannot know Itself as the Subject, except through an object, which in this case would be all of manifested reality. So Source has a dream that is the object of this knowing itself, and that is all of manifested appearance. In this dream we, the individual body/mind organisms, are not the *dreamer* but the *dreamed*. And like all energy that pulses, Source has this dream on a breath-like pulsation: Creation on the inbreath and dissolution and rest on the outbreath. If you want to believe the *Bhagavad Gita*,[2] God's inbreath and outbreath each last for a duration of 311 trillion, 40 billion years of earth time, and this pulsation goes on for eternity.

Now this is where a more intimate and personal understanding of Source at rest and Source in manifestation came through in the voice of my deliverance. At rest, Source is the very epitome of unlimited, infinite power, awareness, and bliss. The one and only thing that Source doesn't have is LIMITATION! And so evolved my Freedom/Limitation resolution.

We have all had dreams whereby we are in big trouble; the bad guys are after us, our feet are seemingly stuck, and we can't even cry out for help. If we happen to have a gun, instead of shooting, the bullets just fall out of the barrel. We wake up shaking, in cold sweats, relieved out of our mind that it was just a nightmare of a dream and life is not really limited like that. This is analogous to what happens to Source. It also dreams that It is limited through this universe of appearance, and through individual mind/body organisms, that illusion is personified.

This dream has all the reality for Source that our dreams have for us. The Source dream is complete with every kind of limitation imaginable: wars, famine, pestilence, child abuse, pain, suffering, pollution, death, and so on and on. As each individual mind/body organism dies and goes back into beingness, there is a cessation of the individual dream, and Source feels "Ah! All that limitation isn't real after all! I am infinite in every way!" And so the drama of Source, amusing Itself by dreaming dreams of limitation, goes on until the next outbreath when It rests in absolute quietness again until the next inbreath.

When you as an individual have a dream of violence, did you really kill that other person? Were you really stabbed through the heart? During the dream you would say, "Of course." But on awakening, you know it to be all illusion within the dream and no one died or was hurt. It is the same situation within the dream of Source. But with one big difference! So it doesn't get out of hand and become unbearable like our sleeping dreams can get at times, Source has put a safety-valve factor in our waking dream in order to ensure that it stays amusing. I call this safety-valve factor the Freedom/Limitation equation. It goes like this: For every bit of limitation or contraction experienced in a situation, there is an equal and compensatory balance factor of freedom or expansion also experienced. This Freedom/Limitation balance is not only true of each individual life, but also every situation in that life and every event in the whole universe. In other words, it is never more than you can bear overall, because in addition to the Freedom/Limitation factor, there is always the ultimate exit door out of this dream and back to Source, the ultimate safety net called death.

A quick and easy personal example of this would be the limitation caused by being incarcerated under oppressive and inhuman conditions balanced by the freedom within prison to experience alone time, without serious responsibility, and to explore the inner world of Spirit. A national example would be the limitation of war balanced by the freedom experienced as everyone drops previous prejudices and works together in harmony against a common enemy. Every crisis, big or small, creates a different perspective on life thereafter.

So, for the individual body/mind organism existing on planet Earth, there is no purpose or goal except to be a vehicle through which Source can amuse itself by experiencing limitation in this Leela, or Divine Comedy of Life. Because of the Freedom/Limitation equation in our existence, this reduces every single possible event or situation in our lives to a common denominator, which is that EVERY SITUATION IS THE SAME, SO IT DOESN'T REALLY MATTER IN THE LONG RUN HOW IT TURNS OUT!!!

As part of the Leela, we are faced with horrendous choices in life:

Do I marry this person or that one?
Do I become a doctor or a pilot?

Do I end my life when I have a terminal disease
or do I suffer through it?
Do I get an abortion or keep the child?

The Freedom/Limitation equation assures us that either choice that is made by Source (we don't choose, we just think we do) will result in an equal amount of Freedom/Limitation. Whether we go left or right, or stay in the middle, when we come to a fork in the road, the end results are the same for us as individuals and for Source, who made the decision anyway and who enjoys either outcome. Everyone's life at the end is the same, no better or worse than any other, in spite of what appearances may dictate. Always remember that God has no favorites, and no one has an advantage or disadvantage over anyone else, since it is all Source anyway.

[1] Satchitananda: Literally: existence (knowledge or awareness), bliss.

[2] *Bhagavad Gita:* A Hindu scripture. The basic directions for a spiritual life as spoken by Krishna, the Supreme Lord, to his disciple Arjuna.

CHAPTER 7

THE ROLE OF THE EGO PERSONALITY

When Source expands from the state of rest in the unmanifest, to create the manifest world of appearance, It endows the creature called human with a feature distinct from all others—an intellect. The main function of this intellect is to be a receiver of thought from Subject Source to object human. The brain is not a transmitter and cannot have original thoughts on its own as a function of the ego personality, only that which it receives from Source. Another unique function of the brain is to simultaneously receive and place the thought into a system of built-in polarity. For example, a person walks out the door and experiences the temperature outside. This temperature is then compared with previous temperatures and judged as hot. Then another judgment as perhaps too hot. Then a critical analysis of the consequences of a ride in the non-air-conditioned car to work. Because the brain was designed this way by Divine Intent, we live in a world of constant dualism that judges everything by various degrees of polarity: good versus bad, right versus wrong, hot versus cold, up versus down. This function of judging all thoughts and sensations conditions in the individual mind/body organism a mistaken belief that he/she is the subject and all others are the objects of their thoughts. This also causes the individual to feel separate from all others in the universe and from the Source of which he/she actually is the full essence and expression. But Source has come through Its infinite intelligence in this design of the intellect in order to create the very playing fields of limitation that It seeks with such an insatiable quest. And because every single mind/body organism has a unique personality that we call the ego, or that I call the "me" in contrast to the "I" of Source, we see how Source has at least six billion different experiences of limitation each moment, and that's only on Earth.

Without the automatic response of a judgment to a thought, usually a negative one, which then causes the contraction of limitation, there would be no Divine Leela at play here. Imagine a world without judgments, comparisons, opinions and preferences! Everyone perfectly attuned to Consciousness as the Source and feeling the Oneness instead of his/her own separation. No drama, no conflicts, no story line to get immersed in as though this were all real and not a dream. No egos fighting for dominance or recognition or revenge. No more dualism, because the duality of the opposite polarities is seen as interconnecting sides that meet in the middle and cancel each other out. In other words, where all humans see and feel themselves as Pearls of pure Consciousness and no longer use their onion vision through their multilayered conditioning. We are talking about total awakening to the original state of enlightenment and a world without limitation, which leaves only freedom. What's wrong with this picture? You got it! This is a picture of Source back at rest again in infinite freedom, only now within a perfect world of appearance in the creation. Remember the whole purpose of Source at rest was to create the world of appearance as the outlet for Its insatiable quest for limitation. It only allows freedom to exist alongside limitation as a balance point so that the whole experience doesn't get out of hand.

So from time immemorial, we have spiritual and psychological teachers urging their students to get rid of the ego as the enemy to enlightenment. They may be right in a relative sense, but . . . you can't get rid of ego by intentional effort! Fighting the ego with the ego only serves to strengthen it. And if the ego gets erased by Source as a consequence of Grace and Destiny, then you have Source deprived of one less experience of limitation, because without ego, there is only Oneness without separation and that is freedom only—no limitation involved.

So why would Source allow some individual mind/body organisms to fully awaken and end their journey of limitation? Because of this perfect balance of the Freedom/Limitation equation for the whole planet that we have been discussing here. Source keeps the bell curve of the Freedom/Limitation equation in balance with a few totally ignorant souls at one end, a few awakened souls at the other end, and most of the rest of the players somewhere in the middle. This may come as quite a shock to those New Agers out there who believe the whole planet is rapidly rising in higher consciousness, in fact, even becoming light bodies in the fifth dimension. I don't think so! What would the whole planet waking up at once do to the overall Freedom/Limitation equation on the planet? And even if Source decided to have one totally awakened planet, the shift toward limitation would have to shift to some other negative, dark shadow planet in order to balance out the Universe. So far in the recorded history of the world, we have always had the *modus operandi* of planet Earth engaged in wars, famines, plagues, and man's inhumanity to man as vehicles of limitation.

We have certainly advanced in technology, but spiritual evolution hasn't raised significantly, if we take the criterion of man knowing he is not the doer and the fact that nothing is accomplished by intentional effort. All we have to do is stay in touch with the media to know that this 20th Century was the bloodiest one yet. Over 50 million people were slaughtered in World War II alone. We find the cure for one disease and another more incurable one pops up. What you see here is great fodder for the loose cannon of limitation, alive and well.

However, the role of the ego personality here is the balancing factor, along with Grace and Destiny, in how you proceed to integrate and understand what we are talking about in this story. On the one hand, we have the human predicament that is entirely caused and continues to be strengthened by this phenomenon called the ego personality. On the other hand, we have Grace now dissolving these multilayers of conditioning that the ego personality has built up since birth, just by the fact that we are being exposed to this matter.

Every piece of academic, scientific, scriptural, spiritual or metaphysical knowledge you have ever acquired has thus far contributed to the strengthening of your ego personality. And why is that? Because the majority of all conventional wisdom in the world today stresses the separation of God and man, man and man, man and all other creation. It stresses that you are the doer and responsible for yourself, your loved ones, and the planet. This mind-set has set up and sustained the human predicament in which we find ourselves smack dab in the middle.

Now along comes a mad man who obviously has been hanging out in a bad scene out of *One Flew over the Cuckoo's Nest*[1] for too long. He claims to have been awakened from this mad dream of the human predicament. He bases his experience of total freedom on the understanding that he is not this ego personality that resides in a bag of skin for a limited time frame. In fact, he claims that Source is all there is. Period! That means that what we refer to as the ego part of the personality is really just an illusion being dreamt by Source as some exercise in the Divine Leela of the human predicament.

So how do you think the individual ego personality is going to respond to this challenge to evaporate into the realm of being just a dreamlike, illusionary prop of Source's play? Why, as you can expect, it is going to fight back in its self-survival mode with everything it has that keeps it going and separate: fear, disgust, skepticism, doubt, revulsion, incredulity, horror.

And bear in mind that this is in the natural mode of how it was designed by Source to function in order to keep this Maya[2] and Leela alive. To believe and understand these statements would mean the death and disappearance of the ego. But this may be going against the grain of every experience in your whole life. I think that is why traumatic events tend to stun and nullify the rigid structure of the ego, at least enough for the logical side of the intellect to shut down and the intuitive, creative side to open to Grace and the possibility of other realities not yet experienced in the realm of Spirit. That's what happens sometimes, even on a good psychedelic trip. But that trip can't make a permanent change or dent in the ego. It's a door that slams shut as soon as it opens for a peek at freedom.

What is needed to overcome a whole lifetime of conditioning and ego personality is the Grace to arrive at a point where we just give up all conventional wisdom with its specious answers to the problems of our human predicament. We need the Grace to just surrender the power of the individual "doer" to the understanding that Source is the only movement in the lawful unfolding of manifest destiny.

Do not feel like the Lone Ranger here if you are feeling a little overwhelmed and confused by all of this. The ego personality is not normally going to just lie down and die during a peaceful reading of a little story. But read on in the knowledge that a seed has been planted that Grace can and will water since you have made it this far into this tale of madness and total freedom.

[1] *One Flew over the Cuckoo's Nest:* United Artists, 1975.

[2] Maya: The illusive power of the Source; the veiling and projection of the universe. Illusory world.

2

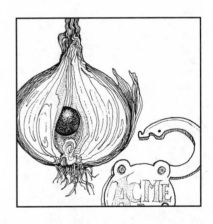

EXPLORING FAMILIAR CONCEPTS

CHAPTER 8

FREE WILL VERSUS PREDESTINATION

Perhaps the greatest obstacle to those of you running around with your head stuck in the tiger's mouth of awakening is breaking through the big, fat, juicy layer of conditioning centered around your free will and intentional efforts at life. It sure feels like you were born with free will. Everything you've learned about New Age awareness says that you are responsible for your thoughts and actions, that thoughts create reality, and that energy follows thought. That you should take responsibility for your life and improve it on all levels: spiritual, emotional, physical, intellectual, cultural, sexual, artistic, and so on. Remember it is with infinite intelligence and wisdom that Source makes the dream we live in so real, and that it's hard to argue with our seeming illusions of free will. And that's by Divine design! It is the intentional efforts of the "me" ego to improve, change, make better, and ameliorate your life conditions that keep limitation alive and well.

There is one aspect of free will allowed, though: the freedom to think you have free will. But this in no way changes the actual truth that you are simply not the *doer*. You are being *done* at every moment by Source. You don't exist as separate from Source except in your fantasy of separation. There is no you as "me." There is only Consciousness as "I AM" in appearance and "I–I" at rest. Your efforts to change life from what it is—as is, into something different are futile. You are headed down the path of destiny that was laid out at the moment of your conception. If you accomplish some planned goal in your life, it is a coincidence because the plan was already established by

Grace and Destiny. It happened in spite of you and not because of you. Source is very cleverly keeping you confused about who's in charge here. Once you awaken and it sinks in that all there is, is Consciousness, and you as the "me" are not the doer, then only one course of nonaction remains open for you to relax into, that is, just be—do nothing—understanding is all!

Once this understanding deepens and becomes part of your Pearl Vision, the deliverance unfolds with a "what is–as is" approach to living life.

CHAPTER 9

WHAT IS – AS IS

This is the buzzword of awakened awareness. Whatever Source has created in the world of appearance is perfect as is, from the perspective of Consciousness. There is purpose and infinite intelligence in every quark of every particle that makes up the universe. The Maya, or illusion, that results from man's capacity to reason is that man can't see the design or purpose in every event from his finite perspective. So as objects enter his senses, or thoughts are received by the brain, judgment forms that results from a comparison of the good and bad of it. This duality doesn't exist in the view of Source because everything serves Its design. We think that perhaps events are created to facilitate the path of the individual. But it is the other way around. Individuals are created to facilitate some event in the design of Consciousness. One of the by-products of an awakened state is to simply view every event as an extension of Consciousness and embrace what is – as is. No judgment, no comparison, no opinion about it, and no preference for how it should be.

In my deliverance, when I experience a critical passing thought or see a contracting situation, I hear the inner voice of deliverance whisper "Namaste." This is an ancient Sanskrit word that roughly means "the Divine in me recognizes and salutes the Divine in you."[1] Instantly, what started out as old onion vision now changes into Pearl Vision and my being embraces whatever is causing the limitation to relax and allow what is to be, be. No need now to make it better, or make it go away, or bring it in closer. My being just feels like a silent witness in choiceless awareness.

Since we are not the doers and intentional efforts have no place in the real world of illusion, this process of allowing, accepting, and embracing what is—as is cannot be practiced as a goal or path. An event either happens by Grace as an experience of freedom or at the opposite polarity, in which case Source gets to pretend that It is feeling limitation again through Its extension—you! As the understanding of Pearl Vision deepens, the experience of what is—as is becomes a normal way of life without a thousand interruptions a day from the voice of deliverance reminding you. So, even though repeating a mantra to intentionally connect with Spirit can be futile, when it happens by Grace, it is very effective. What is—as is! Namaste!

[1] This is usually done by joining the hands as in prayer, bowing slightly, and touching the fingertips to the forehead.

CHAPTER 10

KARMA AND REINCARNATION

These two concepts have been favorite topics for Eastern mysticism and New Age awareness. Their basis of existence is, that man is separate from Source, has an independent existence, and uses his free will and choice to sin or do good, and, as such, he is punished or rewarded, here or in the next life. Typical onion vision, conditioned for thousands of years by religions, scripture, and the prophets.

When we get back to the basics of Pearl Vision, we see that man only thinks and acts as Source designs. Source is the subject; man and all else are the objects. Even though subject and object are one, objects do not act independently of the subject. So the whole notion that man could effect good or evil on his own, independent of Source, or that there even is such a reality as good or evil, doesn't fly in the light of Consciousness. Even further removed from reality is the idea that man would be punished or rewarded by his God for an act he didn't choose to do in the first place.

Now to really get way out there in illusion, we bring in the concept that this lifetime isn't sufficient for all the punishments or rewards of our actions, so we extend it out to countless lifetimes in the future or past to compensate further. Actually, man is so conditioned to believe in himself as a separate self, and so hates the idea of death, that reincarnation provides the perfect backdrop for the immortality of the separate self—the "me."

Karma[1] is handy to relieve high anxiety about those who do bad things to good people, finally getting their "just desserts." Thus the popularity of the phrase "What goes around, comes around." Even if they don't get it in this life, as evil ones often seem to prosper, at least they will get it in the next one.

Karma and reincarnation are terms of purposeful disinformation that Source cleverly uses to perpetuate the field of limitation. They keep alive the greatest source of limitation—the existence of the separate self. Once man is conditioned to feel independent, then the human predicament of actually being powerless and never knowing the why or when of events, to say nothing of the constant change, all work together to cause constant and uninterrupted limitation—the original quest of Source.

So Pearl Vision says there is no karma or personal self to blame, praise, or be reborn. Sorry about that!

---

[1] Karma: Action involved in cause and effect.

THE POWER OF POSITIVE THINKING

This is a concept of onion vision that among the New Agers has certainly become a favorite over the last generation. We have all read enough books and attended enough seminars to know how to get what we want out of life. Any dummy knows that as you think, so you become. That the thought is the father to the deed. Energy follows thought. So we religiously define our wants, lay out our goals, get our priorities in order, and set up our practice of positive affirmations to cinch the deal. But the trouble is, all we set up is a high level of expectation, which is in direct correlation to the level of disappointment that follows.

As illusionary independent "me's," we want to be in control of our lives and needs. By using the power of positive thinking and affirmations, we think we establish some sort of control over the vagaries of life. We all know people who plan where they want to be in life in 5, 10, or 25 years and then go ahead and follow an itinerary to achieve this.

Pearl Vision, which sees from the perspective of Consciousness, knows that the individual mind/body organism doesn't have a path or a goal in life. Only Source as the subject has a purpose. Objects as vehicles of Source, the Subject, don't have individual purposes. But here again, we see how cleverly Source has conditioned the objects to think they are the subjects who live independently, have goals, and use positive thinking to connect with these goals. This sets up hopes and expectations, which often turn into disappointments, which in turn cause massive contractions or limitations. And there's Source, playing out these fantasies of limitation, because it feels so good to wake up from the dream and realize that It is really Source at rest and unlimited and infinite in every capacity.

Pearl Vision also sees that no matter how much intentional effort is put into a goal, not only is it irrelevant, it is also futile. If the end result happens to turn out the same as the goal of all your positive thinking, then it only happened in spite of you, never because of you. And all those strong, clear, and positive affirmations you made were only the thoughts of Source anyway.

CHAPTER 12

PRAYER

For those of you who don't happen to be conditioned by the power of positive thinking, there's another version of it that's far more acceptable for getting what you want out of life, and that is prayer. Even avowed atheists who find themselves in imminent danger of death or experiencing unbearable pain have been known to reach out and call on God for help. Again, look at the conditioning: Man, separate from God—helpless—dependent on a moody, unknowable but powerful creator. What else can you do in a situation like this? Prayer is used to connect you to this God to get what you want, in case God is not paying attention to all your needs. Just a reminder, you know! Of course, tithing increases your chances of God hearing you. A few sacrifices offered up don't hurt the situation either. If all else fails, make a last-minute promise to God that you will change and really be good this time if He gives you what you desire.

Pearl Vision sees the infinite intelligence of Source located within each quark of the universe (a quark being the smallest known particle yet discovered by quantum physicists). But each quark of Consciousness is a hologram of the entire Source. Every quark is connected to every other quark to form just one infinitely intelligent Whole. Compare this to the cells in your body, each one moving independently of the others, but all acting for the good of the whole. Your DNA in the cells also separately contains the hologram of the whole purpose and nature of the body.

So prayer or supplication to someone outside yourself is irrelevant to what has already been designed in perfection and is now in the process of a lawful unfolding of manifest destiny. Prayer is just another clever trick of Source to play the game of limitation because it emphasizes what you are lacking, hope to get, and probably won't, thus causing another contraction from disappointment.

But there is an aspect of prayer that has come to my attention since the wake-up call. I have been describing the rapture where one is usually swept away in powerful currents of freedom, peace, and joy. Another aspect of this rapture is an overwhelming moment-to-moment feeling of gratitude, which is very akin to prayer. Each breath is a deep "Ahhh!" of profound gratitude for the experience of such oneness with Source, relief that the conflict and confusion are now over and one can relax into no more doing, just being, and reveling in this deliverance that deepens the understanding daily.

This gratitude of which I speak does not mean that the "me" is so fortunate as to have won this universal lottery of awakening. No, there is no "me" home now to enjoy anything. There is just awareness that the "I," as in "I Am That," is the "I" of Consciousness at rest and Consciousness in appearance, and they are one and the same Source. In Pearl Vision, the only prayer worthwhile and meaningful is the prayer of gratitude, singing out in joy at the awesome diversity of the One in the many.

I remember my last prayer of supplication to God, whomever that might be. It happened about six weeks before the wake-up call and I had pretty much resigned myself to never understanding this whole spiritual evolution trip. The problem I was experiencing then was that having to be in prison, I was living in the midst of incredible violence, hostility, and hatred, to the point where I began to wonder if some of the inmate souls had ever made it yet to even a human level of awareness. All I could do was to cry out daily from the depths of my anxiety about survival here: "Please God, grant me the vision and true understanding of this so-called "Oneness" of the universe that the spiritual masters are always describing in their awakened states." The next thing I knew, there came the wake-up call and the ever present experience of this yearned for "Oneness." Now I am not presuming that my last fervent prayers for Oneness were effective and prompted God to bend His Will. I am just saying that I happened to be at that fork in the road of the lawful unfolding of my manifest destiny. Grace, Destiny— right time at the right place, prayer. Guess which word here has become one of those irrelevancies of onion vision?

CHAPTER 13

THE ROLE
OF DREAMS

Source has done a pretty good job of locking us all into a state of illusionary separation. This is accomplished nicely by giving us an intellect whose main function is to receive the thoughts of Source and then separate them into the duality of opposites, to then choose one of the polarities as good or bad. This whole process of separation is then securely reinforced by the multiple layers of conditioning that our original pure Pearl of Consciousness gets all wrapped up in by just being alive.

There are seekers reading this book who are ready to be finders in the process of awakening back to their original state of innocence. So it seems to me that if you can intellectually understand the concepts laid out here so far and allow them to percolate on down to the heart over time, that is the most probable scenario for you to explode at some point into an intuitive knowing that becomes your wake-up call.

I have found that by studying the nature of dreams before and after awakening, they have helped me to intellectually understand the nature of Consciousness. Now I don't mean understanding the symbolic nature of events in dreams, like what it means when I run around naked. That psychological analysis is just another story within the story. I mean how dreams function. Surely Source has given us a key of understanding here if we can see it.

In our human dreams, we are in our bed at night at rest. Once we fall asleep, from seemingly out of nothing there appears a reality that, though we know it is only an illusion, sure feels real to all our senses and emotions. Dramas involving the deepest expression of love or fear, with all their accompanying side-kicks, are lived and played out. People often get hurt, tortured, and even slaughtered at will. You, as a gentle, evolved soul in your waking life, do things in dreams that are unspeakable.

When you wake up from a nightmare, was anybody really hurt, really killed, really raped or abused? No, it was all an illusion! When you were stuck in a nightmare where vicious dogs were at your throat, your feet were stuck in mud, your voice couldn't call for help, weren't you relieved and excited when you suddenly awoke in a cold sweat and found that this was just a dream and you are not limited like that? It felt good to hug your pillow then, for the intensity of the nightmare dream added to the freedom and safety you felt in your secure little bed.

Are you getting the connection here as to what Consciousness at rest is doing in the world of appearance? As above, so below! At times Consciousness is at rest, dwelling in Its infinite vastness—eternal, aware, and at peace. Then for a change of pace, It periodically creates a world of appearance through a dreamlike process in which It becomes the Subject of that object, though It remains one with it. In this dreamlike, illusionary reality that exists only in the world of thought energy, the Subject is able to experience through Its objects a Leela of limitation, the one quality It doesn't have in Its infinite arsenal. But in this dream, Source gets to experience six billion times a day the intense experience of limitation and no two of them alike. And that's just through the humanoids on planet Earth. Throw in the quasi-infinite number of plant and animal life expressions of limitation and the experience heats up. Now add on all the other galaxies and we are talking big-time experience!

But when the dream ends and all the bubbles that we are on the fabric of being finally dissolve back into Beingness at rest, was anyone really hurt? Did we really die, or was it like our own dream characters? In a dream this real and intense, imagine how great it has to feel to know that the limitation was only imagined. And because of the equal balance of freedom alongside of the limitation in the equation, it was all bearable and highly amusing.

It seems that Source, the Subject, allows dreams to happen in Its objects so they can more easily understand the whole process of the Divine Leela, and how important it is that Maya be realistic to be effective.

Understanding the nature of dreams also helps to put the concepts of time and space in better perspective. In a dream, you have a long sequence of events that within the framework of the dream feels like forever. Yet, studies done in dream labs with REM (rapid eye movement) technology have established that your whole dream took place in only a few seconds. And those mountains and trees in your dreams, how long did they take to be created? And all that space you were hanging out in, where did it come from, and where did it go? So based on the analogy of time and space in dreams, just how real do you think they are in the waking dream also?

Another dream phenomenon that occurred for about a year before my awakening was that I began to have lucid dreams for the first time in my life. I would be in a dream and wake up within the dream knowing that it was all just a dream. In fact, I could really enjoy the dream, no matter which direction it took. At first, I would direct the dream in the direction that I wanted it to go, and sure enough, my imagination would create the total outcome. But after experimenting with this, I quickly realized that allowing the dream to unfold on its own and just hanging out with it as a witness, albeit a lucid witness who knew it was only a dream, somehow made the dream far more enjoyable and varied than the directed dreams.

There were two benefits from lucid dreaming for me besides being the most enjoyable journeys I ever made in my head space. One: Allowing what is to be as is without changing anything (like a passenger), was better than driving the dream bus with directions. Very valuable lesson in life! Two: The incredible awareness that happens when you wake up in the dream state and see through all the make-believe served as a presentiment of what was to happen later, when I woke up in the waking state as well. The parallels are almost identical. I don't have lucid dreams much anymore, but every day is a lucid walk through the dream world of the waking, living, personal dream. This lucid dreamlike awareness is continual, and is another by-product of the rapture.

There is yet another curiosity about my dream life that I can relate to you. Ever since my awakening, whatever degree of consciousness that is present through the deliverance in my waking state is also present to the same degree in my dream state. So it seems to me that the deliverance is continuing at full force during my dream state as well as my waking state. There is never the confusion or conflict in dreams anymore that was rampant before the awakening. Nightmares are a thing of the past. I deal with situations in dreams the same way I would in waking life.

Pearl Vision sees all of waking reality as an ongoing dream of an equal balance of freedom and limitation, over in the blink of an eye, and most blissful when allowed to unfold without intentional efforts. When it seems most intense and real, then you know Source is having a great time amusing Itself through your vehicle, and that is the only reason we are here!

I must admit that when folks first hear my explanation of Source "amusing" Itself through us, many are freaked out. "How morbid, how cruel!" And their reaction is understandable because their perspective comes from the third dimension rather than the broad and transcendental view of the fourth. If you still see Source as separate from each and every one of us, then, of course, it would be cruel to be amused at someone else's expense. But there is no separation here. There is only Source projecting out into multiple diverse appearances, each one reflecting a unique and different experience of life in the third dimension. Instead of Source being at rest, It is now active and infinitely creative in a dream world of appearance as It gets the most experience possible out of every single life event.

When Source feels the drama of the human predicament with all its contractions, limitations, and infinite diversity, the overall sensation comes closest to our English word *amusement*. It is experienced with great humor and a sense of aliveness in contrast to Its normal state of infinite expansion at rest. We don't yet have detailed enough words to adequately express this phenomenon, but the dictionary defines *amusement* as engaging the attention in manner that keeps one interested or engrossed in a laughter-provoking, light, or frivolous way. Sure sounds like Source to me! Amusement only makes perfect sense when you feel the Oneness rather than the separation.

In the third dimension, everything in relation to God is felt as oh so serious. In the fourth dimension, my experience of how Source operates is all playful, amusing, and with an infinite sense of humor in Its diversity. Maybe the old concept of Jehovah conditioned our minds to regard God as anything but playful or amusing unto Itself. But I have to tell you, this is the quintessence of Source in my story.

THE
ASCENSION

This concept is one of the hot buzzwords of the New Age and one that had me quite excited before the wake-up call. In case you are in old, conventional wisdom where ascension still means going up to heaven with Jesus at the second coming, I'll explain the modern version of it. Some New Agers believe that the whole planet is moving into another dimension, from the third to the fourth. It's moving there because we are at the time in the planetary evolution of the earth to raise the consciousness to enlightenment level. This ascension is coming in three successive waves for the chosen ones, and the rest have to go live on some other denser planet of low-life consciousness and work out their bad karma. When you ascend, you exchange your old, worn-out, physical, dense body for a new fifth-dimensional, immortal light body that travels right through solid objects and moves at the speed of thought. In some versions of the ascension, you get orientated to this changeover in a massive space ship somewhere up there that is hundreds of miles in diameter.

While sitting in that "black hole of Calcutta," the county jail, the whole idea of the New Age ascension sounded pretty awesome to me, especially the part about passing through walls. But the reality sank in after awakening that the whole concept of the ascension is just another hype by Source to trick us into hoping for a better state of affairs than just being with what is—as is!

Look at all the limitation mileage it gets out of millions of New Agers contracting into limitation when this thing doesn't come off as advertised. In addition to the New Age version of the ascension, we also have a Christian version of it, dear to another one-and-a-half-billion Christians. In this one, Jesus is coming back for them, and whether dead or alive, they are all ascending into heaven together. If I ever told all those Christians that I think Jesus melted back into Beingness again at the moment of death, never to return to planet Earth or anywhere else again, I suspect I would meet a demise similar to the one that Jesus experienced.

Pearl Vision sees the concept of the Ascension as the same as any other attempt by the separated ego to ameliorate conditions in life as we know it on Earth. The ascension offers hope of a way out of this. But Consciousness is all there is, either at rest or in appearance. If you are Source in appearance, then whether you have a third or fifth-dimensional body, you are still limited by being in manifestation. Living in a light body would bring its very own set of limitations with it to counter-balance the freedom it offers. This Freedom/Limitation equation applies to ego personality in any dimension and to all of the phenomenal world of appearance. The very optimal situation for us already here in this dimension is what is—as is, until that also changes—and changes are guaranteed to be constant.

CHAPTER 15

THE ROLE OF CONSTANT CHANGE

When we become aware that we are in a physical body, we are faced with two absolute certainties: constant change and ultimate death. What role does change play in this Leela we call life on earth? If we bear in mind that Source is in an insatiable quest for limitation as a contrast to Its infinite expansion, then change begins to make sense. Within the human predicament, man's nature can be extremely resilient. He has a potential to quickly adapt his spirit to whatever catastrophe he may find himself in. What was too horrible yesterday becomes just so-so today and normal by tomorrow. The same holds true for any serendipitous bonanza that befalls him. It too quickly becomes a normal situation, no longer holding the initial allurement. So in It's infinite wisdom, Source has introduced the wild card of constant change to keep the limitation alive and well; otherwise things could get pretty boring and uneventful. We all want the consistency and security of everything remaining the same. After all, how else would we be able to delude ourselves that we're in control here? But when everything keeps changing on us, we have to be constantly vigilant. Even the quantum physicists know that without change, the universe would collapse. In fact, they now have a theory of how chaos maintains perfect order in the universe.

Have you noticed how many people seem to fear and resist changing the *status quo*? At the first hint of coming changes, they feel contraction, the very essence of limitation. So this is how the balance works in the Freedom/Limitation equation: We finally adapt to new circumstances, begin to feel comfortable, and then—change comes in and we are off to the races again.

Pearl Vision sees the hand of Source in all changes. It's just another opportunity to say "Namaste" to the Leela of life.

CHAPTER 16

SPIRITUAL DISCIPLINES

In our illusion of being in control of our life and destiny, we become seekers, frantic to attain higher consciousness or enlightenment. It's a built-in condition of maintaining our separate sense of identity from Source. The ways we try to coax Grace out of God are endless, so I'll just hit on the major movers.

Eastern mysticism focuses the spiritual disciplines in seeking through these expressions:

> Service to others.
> Satsang[1]—This means getting together with other seekers and sharing your truth and experiences.
> Meditation—A *sine qua non* to knowing God.

The New Agers' approach may be best summed up by perhaps reading an Esalen catalogue of self-improvement courses or understanding what I went through in that phase.

So when Pearl Vision looks at spiritual disciplines, it keeps the following information in mind: Consciousness is all there is. The individual mind/body organism is not the doer. Whatever happens to you in your quest for God through your practices depends on your destiny and Grace.

There is no magic formula for awakening. If and when it is your time to wake up, it will happen. Nothing can stop it—nothing can help it. There's nothing to do that makes any difference one way or the other. There's not even a necessity to wake up. Source is playing at limitation through each and every one of us. It has an equal, but differently distinct, experience whether it practices 16 hours of zazen[2] meditation a day in a Zen monastery, or is a Hutu soldier in Africa daily slaughtering Tutsis. Each is a perfect expression of Source in manifestation pretending It is limited.

It seems to me that man is interested in seeking out God because deep within his inner knowing is the remembrance that his essence really is pure Consciousness. But he looks out through these myopic eyes and finite intellect, sees himself trapped in a limited body, and panics. He feels his separation from Source and fears that he is trapped forever and will never get back. And so begins his quest to find his way home again. This is as it should be—all included in the Divine design of the dream of limitation.

Pearl Vision knows that there is no need to find your way back to God. You already are that which you are seeking. Nothing needs to be done about awakening. If you are destined for awakening, it will happen on its own in its own good time, not because of you, but in spite of you. It seems like there is a natural progression from being a nonseeker to seeking, and then to finding. It seems to be centered around quiet time and meditation. It seems to involve teachers who pass on their understanding. All of wisdom is contained within the essence of each and every one of us. When we center, or listen to this inner voice in quiet time, then Satsang becomes nonstop, straight from the Source. Relax into the knowing that there is no mysterious formula or magic key to attaining the Godhead. You already are that, so you can't screw it up or lose out. Maybe you will die awakened, and maybe you won't!

It's all the same experience once our bubbles of appearance in the fabric of being pop and we melt back into Source, the dream of separation having ended. And no matter what role we play in this dream of appearance, it is all the same also. Each life and each separate situation is perfectly balanced with the Freedom/Limitation equation. So it doesn't matter whether you get to play priest or barbarian. Inside of your being, as you are acting the role out, there is equal balance in both. This is why, if you do wake up, you spend the first few months of deliverance laughing your head off at the cosmic joke of it all. You finally get to watch Source perpetrating conventional wisdom as purposeful disinformation to keep Its illusion alive.

In my own experience of living in awareness of who I am—I Am That—almost all former practices have fallen away. Meditation has simply become quiet time when the understanding of this Pearl Vision deepens. I no longer watch my breath, my posture, or my thoughts. Instead I just purr like a contented cat with the Ahhhh! experience that life is good! Ahhhh! All is well! Ahhhh! Nothing to do! Ahhhh! Just be! Ahhhh! Understanding is all! Ahhhh! What is–as is! Everything is as it should be!

Does this sound like hard work? Hardly! No more reading any books, spiritual, scientific, or even stories about the story. Words, whether written or spoken, somehow weigh heavy on the sacredness of the moment. They hurt! No more words are necessary. The rapture of being swept away is more than sufficient, and this rapture is ever-present now.

I find I don't ask for anything anymore. If Source wants to give it, it comes without asking. I also find I can't refuse anyone anymore. If Source wants something, It asks me through the requests of others. Also, owning anything at all anymore feels so unnecessary, even burdensome. Whatever I need mysteriously shows up in abundance. There are no longer any goals or paths to attract or motivate me. Life is good—just as it is. And because I'm not planning for it anymore, it's a wonderful surprise when it suddenly changes and fresh new material shows up.

Workshops and seminars hold no interest as part of the self-help information-gathering process. The same for self-help books, tapes, and videos. With the awakening, the journey for knowledge at all levels has gone from insatiable to totally complete. When this happened, I still had about two dozen new books I hadn't read yet. That's not a lot, considering I had read an average of a book a day for the first two years of lockup. But

when it was clear to me that any more words just felt ponder-
ous, I gave them away and refused any more new ones.

Remember earlier I mentioned that before the wake-up
call, there was always this free-floating anxiety present that I
had to do something terribly important or else, but I never
knew what that was? Now there is the deep peace of knowing
that there is *nothing to do*, whether now or ever! I also mentioned the feeling of imminent doom that was ever present.
That was replaced by a constant mantralike assurance from
Source that is always floating like a sweet-sounding melody
through my head: Consciousness is all there is!

The over-30-year concern about the purity of my diet is
now over. What guilt I would feel if I slipped off my self-
imposed regime of whatever my food fad was at the moment.
Now I know I am not what I eat. The only thing that keeps this
bag of skin alive and functioning is Consciousness. Now if
Source wants to operate through the freedom of a healthy body,
I am motivated to eat healthy foods. And if It wants to feel the
limitation of an overweight, artery-clogged, unhealthy body,
I'll only yearn for junk food. The preference of the separated
ego doesn't have any impact on the final outcome anyway.

My 20-year fascination with hatha yoga has given way to
more conventional fitness training now. I did yoga because I
thought it would help align my chakras[4] and facilitate the rais-
ing of consciousness. After all, yoga was a 5,000-year-old spiritual discipline in India. Surely it had to be a key to that magic
formula I was searching for! In my newfound freedom of
awakening, I settled for some aerobics, strength training, and
several miles a day of just plain ole walking. My love affair
with yoga is now just a healthy respect for those who relish it.

So Pearl Vision sees all spiritual practices and disciplines
as irrelevant to actually attaining the Godhead. The joke of the
matter is, you are already that which you are seeking. If Source
wants to have a unique experience of some particular spiritual
discipline through you, you will be attracted to that practice
regardless. Remember each practice would have its own built-

in equation of Freedom/Limitation, so all serves Source equally well in Its quest for limitation. The bottom line once more is just be—do nothing—understanding is all!

[1] Satsang: Discourse of truth. Association with the wise (sat = truth, sang = community).

[2] Zazen: A posture in meditation of sitting erect on a pillow, eyes open, and watching thoughts instead of engaging with them.

[3] Chakras: Plexus of energy centers located throughout the body.

CHAPTER 17

PAIN AND SUFFERING

We have all been born into the human predicament. One of the mind trips here on earth that can make people crazy with confusion is how to deal with pain and suffering, and why a God of love would even want these present in our universe. This presence of pain and suffering is a very big part of the human predicament. This dilemma gets resolved after awakening. Many awakened ones have given the same response: "Go wake up and then come back and tell me if you see any more pain and suffering from that viewpoint!" But they never seem to explain why the view changes, only "Put yourself in my place and tell me what you see."

When Pearl Vision emerges, you begin to see all of reality through the eyes of Source at rest. Onion vision is that conventional wisdom that only sees from the limited view of an illusionary, separated ego self. At rest, Source is aware, at peace, and completely unlimited in all Its capacity. But that infinite capacity at rest is only in a potential state of the form of manifestation. So Source breathes Itself into form and appearance, and experiences Its infinite, unlimited capacity as a contrast to the opposite polarity of a finite and limited experience. And we are that very form through which Source is able to actually feel and experience limitation through the physical discomfort of pain and the mental anguish of suffering. But they are also limited in intensity. If physical pain becomes too much, we pass out. If mental suffering gets overwhelming, we can get amnesia or even go crazy. The final escape hatch from too much of either is death. And that's why we are not immortal as humans. Imagine being trapped forever in this limited body! And that's also why the Freedom/Limitation equation is built into every situation.

The way Source has this experience of limitation is in the form of a dream. It looks real and it feels real, but it is only a dream in which Source knows Its own unlimited self at rest. And that's why we have dreams. We get to have the same experience of limitation in a nightmare that feels oh so good when we wake in our microcosm that Source does in Its macrocosm.

Pearl Vision deals with pain and suffering as coming directly from Source. It eliminates the whole concept of victimhood. Nobody is out to get us! Not God, not our fellow man as enemy, and not some tragic flaw in our psychological makeup that transforms us into pathetic sadists or masochists. We are all in the middle of the human drama. This drama has a specific script for each actor that was written by Source and handed to us in our DNA at conception. Source takes the role of each player and acts it out to perfection. While this is all happening, Source is also sitting as the audience, immensely enjoying all the emotions that Its drama is producing. When the dream drama is all over, Source takes another outbreath and enjoys Itself at rest for the next exhalation.

So, when we, as individual mind/body organisms, have as our role—in this moment—some particular experience of either pain or suffering, we can know through the awakening and deliverance process the actual significance of it all. Source is actually having this unique and important experience through the lawful unfolding of our manifest destiny. Therefore, I can only accept, allow and embrace what is–as is.

Here are two examples of this. First: pain—the normally unbearable pain of an abscessed tooth. I went to the prison dentist on an emergency basis. He examined me and said it was too infected to work on then, and there weren't any time slots available anyway. He gave me some penicillin and pain pills, and scheduled me back in a week. Even though I have a very low threshold for pain, I experimented. Instead of taking the pain pills, I just allowed the pain to be felt, not changing it or making it better. After all, if Source wants an experience of limitation through a toothache, let's make it a total experience! But to my shock, I discovered that just embracing the pain made it greatly diminish, and I only felt a dull pressure at most. The experience turned into one of total freedom, and the dentist could not believe I lived with the pain for a week without taking the pain killers.

Second: The experience of mental suffering is similar. There occurred several emotional and mental blows to me after the wake-up that, under pre-wake-up conditions, would have normally flattened me into a near clinical depression. However, using the same approach as with pain, that is, accepting rather than resisting, I felt as if I were Source having these unique experiences of limitation. I stayed with the feeling and did nothing to numb it, like working out or doing a no-brainer with the TV (the usual kinds of distractions that formerly worked to ameliorate this kind of situation). The experience was lived as though this were the most important role being played in the universe. Again, like the toothache, it transmuted into another whole dimension of freedom. Who would have ever thought?

Now Pearl Vision isn't embracing these situations "as-is" as a technique to make them better. It is coming from the understanding that we are the Source and, as such, experience what is – as is from that perspective and not from the view of a separated ego self that takes everything as a personal affliction. What the old masters said is true. As unbelievable as it may sound, once you have crossed over to viewing all of reality from the experience of Source, pain and suffering have lost their bite. Their impact is so lessened as to be no longer relevant any more.

CHAPTER 18

AFTERLIFE

Every description of life after death that I've ever heard is from the perspective of a self that is separate from God and maintaining this separate, independent, and autonomous state of being throughout eternity. It doesn't matter which scripture you study or what New Age channel you listen to, most of the scenarios all end up with you, the created, and God, the Creator. Two—not One. This misinformation has been cleverly disseminated by Source to keep up the appearance of duality and the resulting limitations that Source enjoys so much. It makes the dream more real if you have visions of what will be after a guaranteed death as you continue to jog along as the same self, either in another body at some future reincarnation, or as an angel next to God for all eternity. It is still the separated sense of ego that wants perpetuity as the self it now considers itself to be.

Here is the way Pearl Vision sees afterlife. We are like a bubble floating on the surface of the ocean. The bubble has to pop some day. When a bubble pops, it dissolves back into the beingness of ocean that it has always been. Where else can it go? That bubble that popped has no separate identity or any glue holding it together so that it shows up in another place at another time as that very same bubble.

The big question is what does it feel like as an individual to fall back into the beingness of Source? Nobody knows because there are no individual selves to know this experience. There is only the One experience, then, of Source. The experience of Source has been traditionally passed on as "Satchitananda, Eternal reality, aware of Itself, in Bliss!" That's it!

That's the only clue! And that's just hearsay from the masters. But we don't really know for sure just what this experience is because we have limited imagination at this point to figure it out. That's part of the human predicament of not knowing, and the powerlessness to do anything about it.

Does it bother me that we can't possibly know what after-life is all about? Not at all! The present "swept away" experience, as an awakened extension of Source, is such a rapture that ending this dream of illusion and limitation by death can only be an awesome new discovery awaiting that moment. Will we experience Source still in manifestation, or will we revert back to rest again? I love surprises!

CHAPTER 19

FORKS IN
THE ROAD

Our human predicament only includes one freedom of choice, and that is the freedom to think we have free choice. But the reality is that Consciousness is all there is, so Source is making all the moves and decisions, no matter how much it may appear to the contrary. This illusion of us being in control is what fuels the core reactor of our limitation furnace. In our human predicament, a lot of time, energy, angst, and regret are spent in the process of decision making. We come to a fork in the road. Onion vision makes a list of all the pros and cons and measures them one against the other. Then after an agonizing decision is finally made with the head, we go left or right, never knowing if we made the right choice or not.

Pearl Vision gives us a much more laid-back approach to these forks in the road. The way Source seems to function in the human predicament in regard to the available options is to trigger thoughts of the attractiveness of one fork over the other. That's the principal method of stimulation to a particular course of action. When it comes down to that moment of which button to push, we can go with the heart instead of the head. We have full intuitive capacity as an extension of Consciousness. If both options look, feel, and weigh the same and you have to choose now, flip a coin! You can't lose, because the bottom line is that because of the Freedom/Limitation equation built into every situation, the results of either choice as it affects your inner being are the same. You have to choose between marrying Black Bart or Mr. Right, but you are stuck in the middle without a nudge from Spirit. What do you do? Well, you act "as if" you had free will, pick one of the two and know for certain that, as your life and manifest destiny unfolds, either choice would have been the same as an equal balance to your overall experience.

The finger that in great doubt and hesitation pushes the red button instead of the green button is still, and only, the movement, thought, and impulse from Source. All the dickering around in anguish over which button to push is part of the limitation game of Leela. Never forget, this bag of skin and bones is a puppet, and Source directs and pulls the strings.

When I became aware of this particular layer of onion vision peeling away in the deliverance, I experimented a lot with decision making and follow-through. Being in a maximum security prison situation was a great opportunity to experiment without catastrophic effects. Let me give you a couple of examples. We slept 1,300 inmates in a space originally designed for 200 in 1936. So you have a "bunkie," someone who sleeps above or below you. When your bunkie leaves the dorm for whatever reason, conventional wisdom dictates that you better check around and secure someone pronto who is not a psychotic killer, racist, or drug addicted thief to share the 64 cubic feet of space with you for the next indefinite period of time. If you don't shake the bushes and find someone, staff will assign someone (possibly your worst nightmare of a person) to share your limited space.

When Pearl Vision opened up and deliverance kicked in, I went from a doing mode to a stay back and see what happens, nondoing whenever, wherever possible, mode. Without any intentional effort on my part at recruitment, I was constantly amazed how everything got done, in fact, better than if I had gotten involved. People showed up in that empty bunk that were delightful. I learned that being a silent witness to the whole decision-making process, without a preference for the outcome, churned out results that can only be described as miraculous. Day after day, situations would arise about what to do about my legal status with the courts, what to do inside the walls on various inmate programs, and what to do about my family and business situations outside the walls. The solutions were best found in just watching how everything gets done perfectly without personal involvement in the outcome. Even though I had made no decision or intentional effort toward a prison program, I would run into the person in charge of that program by a "chance encounter" and we would start chatting and the next thing I knew, I was all signed up and wondering: "Now, how did that happen?"

I can't tell you the significance of this transition for me from "doing" to "nondoing," and I don't mean nondoing as another form of doing to get better results. I mean nondoing as one would ride an inner tube in a white-water river, just out there getting carried 100 percent by the current, no involvement necessary or possible. All my life before this I had prided myself on overachieving in every endeavor. I was sure that all results were directly linked to my superior decision making and Type-A personality approach to what I focused on. What a pleasant part of the rapture to now just feel swept away instead of swimming upstream in the river of life.

A person caught up in the multilayered conditioning of onion vision just cannot comprehend that life gets lived in the most wondrous, miraculous fashion when all intentional efforts are abandoned to knowing you are That. You are Source—all is well—all is good—it doesn't matter which fork you go down, it's all the same. What matters is understanding this, not doing anything about it. You see, doing becomes irrelevant when you understand that you are not the doer.

CHAPTER 20

WHAT IF YOU WERE APPOINTED CREATOR OF THE PLANET?

As part of our inherited and preconditioned human predicament, many of us look around at planet Earth and think there's something terribly wrong here. Did God screw up with all these mistakes we see? We all think we could do things very differently and by different, we mean better—much better. All right, let's pretend that you are a separate entity from the weird God that created this mess, and this God decides to let you re-create in your own design. Now you get to eliminate the bad stuff like:

>All diseases—starting with cancer and AIDS
>Famine and Homelessness
>Violence
>Pain and Suffering
>War and Strife
>Environmental Pollution
>Crime
>Death and Old Age
>Man's Cruelty to Animals
>Man's Cruelty to Man
>Injustice
>Poverty
>Fear
>Envy
>Rage
>Unhappy Relationships
>Destruction by Nature
>Addictions

I'm sure this list could continue indefinitely. But when you finished with your re-creation of the planet, if you did a thorough job, you would have removed all limitations from the face of the Earth. Everyone would be basically the same, stuck here forever in a boring, saccharin-sweet environment, with an immortal body.

But far more important than that, you have put God as Source into a real predicament. Here you have placed It into a world without limitation but still in the world of appearance. The whole reason for this manifestation in the first place was so that Source could amuse Itself with finite limitation. Now you removed the *raison d'être* of our existence. Source might as well go back to rest and dissolve the whole creation. You get the picture?

We all see with a limited mind, and lacking the perspective of the big picture, no one is capable of knowing what is best for life on Earth as we know it. But Source does know and is using infinite wisdom in keeping this Leela alive and enjoyable. So with Pearl Vision, you wouldn't want to change a single thing in the present agenda on planet Earth. Your deliverance has taught you that the rapture lies in accepting what is—as is! So you are no longer in charge of saving, changing, or making the planet a better place to live for all. If Source wants to use your old bag of skin to accomplish some effect on the planet, you, as the "me" part of ego personality, couldn't stop, help, or slow it down if you wanted to. It will just happen anyway—not because of you, but in spite of you. Doesn't it encourage you to know that no matter what you see about you, all is truly well, and you wouldn't want to change a single detail of this destiny in its manifest unfolding?

CHAPTER 21

WORLD
EVENTS

Keeping up with world events is a whole new ball game since the wake-up call. Onion vision divides media events into the good guys and the bad guys. We want the bad guys to get stopped and punished. We can't imagine their rationale in being terrorists or carjackers and what we don't understand, we repudiate. We have this morbid fascination with the bad things that happen to good people. Maybe seeing their misfortune helps us to appreciate more our good fortune. But most viewing of world events is followed by judgment and opinion, which, as we have been saying all along here, is what keeps the field of limitation alive and well as grist for the Divine mill of Leela.

What a change of experience to watch world news at night and know in your intuitive being that there are no culprits, there is only Source as the perpetrator of events. To watch the incredible drama that unfolds and see how most of those involved believe the normal conditioning about blame, victimhood, and vengeance. Can you imagine the following scenario? A victim of a carjacking is being told by a messenger of God that he should just relax about his lost car, since it was really Source who needed it and took it for a matter of universal balance. "Now, please don't get mad at the violent gang-banger who grabbed it, as he was only being used as an instrument! And don't try to understand the reasons behind this, as it is part of your destiny. And no need to grieve over your loss. And don't resist by shooting the carjacker. All is well!"

That kind of explanation from the Divine messenger, if perfectly understood, would immediately change a highly charged situation of limitation into surfing a wave of freedom all the way home. But the only messenger that Source does send about the real meaning of life and world events is one whose name is "Deliverance." Its role is to change our old, conditioned onion vision into a clear perception of Pearl Vision. Once the clear understanding of Pearl Vision is percolating in the intuitive part of the heart, the rapture naturally follows.

So watching world events has become a kind of Satsang for me, in which the inner voice of Spirit points out the game plan of the Freedom/Limitation equation. What a huge cosmic joke it becomes when you watch how seriously the players get involved in their roles. You can see right through the political posturing of the GOP or observe the Democrats as just a voice box of Source, coming through with new issues to hook 200 million Americans into a contraction of either for or against. Who could take the politicians seriously if everyone knew that, however the issue goes, it doesn't matter—it's all the same anyhow? Everything works out to an even exchange of Freedom/Limitation.

Every single mind/body organism, at the moment of leaving the bubble of appearance behind as it merges into Pure Beingness at the moment of death, has to laugh at the huge joke of it all. The dream has ended, the illusion of separation is over, the Oneness of Source is all there is, and this is the best of all possible scenarios for this particular mind/body organism. That is the kind of experience I'm talking about, when the rapture of Pearl Vision permeates your entire life. All fingers point only to Source. All events are the play of Source. There is nothing to do but be in the witnessing of these events: All is well— life is good!

CHAPTER 22

THE ROLE OF THE TEACHER

Eastern mysticism has always laid a heavy emphasis on the role of the guru[1] in any approach to awakening. Traditionally, you would live with and serve the master for long years, and if he deemed you a worthy candidate, it was only by the grace of the guru that awakening was bestowed. I always got the impression from what I read that there was some esoteric and mysterious formula that only the guru had that would unlock the knowledge and wisdom of enlightenment. Another trick of conditioning!

For Zen Buddhism, it lies in a combination of the master, or roshi,[2] and cracking the imponderable riddle of a koan,[3] starting usually with the Mu koan. By design, koans don't make any logical sense to the mind, so you have to rely on the intuition of the heart to learn what it means. A typical one would be: "What is the sound of one hand clapping?" Each day you report to the roshi and tell him your insights about the koan and he nearly always says "No way!" So you go back to zazen and meditate some more on it. After you finally get the Mu koan down, they break out another 200 juicy koans to work on, and finally 2,000 of the little fellows.

I have lived in a Zen ashram[4] and meditated 13 hours a day on a koan for months at a time. They figure at least three years to crack the first one and then an additional 20 years to finish the others off. You should achieve satori,[5] or its equivalent to the wake-up call by then. Afterwards, you spend 10 more years integrating your newfound wisdom, after which you are sent out to teach others. Does this sound like a lot of hard work to reach what you already are? Does it look like a lot of intentional efforting for satori? Well, obviously Source has a need for experiencing a specific limitation, as 400,000 Zen monks are alive and well on the planet.

I also lived off and on for years in the community of Guru Maharaji in San Antonio, Texas, and many more in Shri Baghwan Rajneesh's small city of Rajneeshpuran in Oregon. It was not the traditional concept of living one on one with the guru, because there were too many of us for that. I only relate it to you in passing, because I got a taste of what the guru expects of his disciples, and I'm trying to put this all into perspective. Don't forget, there were also 11 years of preparation for the Catholic priesthood in a monastery as a background in Western mysticism.

Now all of this intense seeking in all the traditional avenues only left me confused and skeptical. I finally quit guru hopping and gave up on teachers. In all those years, I had never met one single awakened person! Baghwan may have been, but I never got close enough to him to really know for sure. When I would hear his diatribes against the U.S. government and its policies, or see him surrounded by Uzi-toting bodyguards everywhere he went, I was very confused by it all.

However, he did give me a memorable gift once. In 1984, I took sanyas[6] as his disciple and he changed my name to Satyam Nadeen. "Nadeen" means "ocean" in Sanskrit and "Satyam" means "of truth." Actually it would have been much more appropriate for him to have named me "ocean of confusion," or even better, "ocean of resistance." This was the first and last time he ever bestowed the name "ocean of truth" on a sanyasin.[7]

Because it didn't feel like it even applied to me, I never used the name until after my wake-up call, when all of a sudden it felt not only right but right on. The old "me" was dead and gone anyway, and this was a perfect name for my newly regained "original innocence." So while Rajneesh did not give me the magic key to awakening that I was seeking, he at least gave me a good name for when it came along.

No, it took sitting in a dark hole of a jail, surrounded by conditions of unspeakable cruelty for two years, before the life-long darkness of the soul lifted and the light of who I am flooded in. The wake-up had happened on its own without a personal teacher! But that's not to say that all the previous teachers were not the softening or preparation for the wake-up.

So after all this, how do I feel about the role of teachers? Well, I know that they are absolutely indispensable, but in a very limited way only. It is not necessary to live with and serve a master in a slavelike manner to get his grace for awakening. A true guru knows that the only grace of a guru comes from the Guru of Source and that only by the condition of destiny. However, I don't think any human that starts with onion vision (and that basically includes the planet as we know it) is able to break through the enormous restraints of a lifetime of conditioning on his own unless a teacher who is already there tells him who he really is.

Your conditioning tells you that you are an independent entity with free will, separate from Source, and responsible for your own life. A teacher you respect, admire, and most of all believe, tells you that you are an extension of Consciousness—you are not the doer—neither is anyone else the doer—there's no such thing as free will—no intentional effort—so just be—do nothing—understanding is all!

It doesn't seem possible that a human stuck in the human predicament can make that transition from the duality of separation to the Oneness of Consciousness without a teacher telling him it is not only possible, it is also the only reality there is. I mean, who would have thought that we are not responsible for our own life? It sure never occurred to me, because everything I had ever learned taught me otherwise, including my gurus who said it all depended on them to get through the eye of the needle.

I can tell you from experience how utterly simple it is. Because you are already that which you seek (God—Source—Enlightenment), it just takes a wake-up call for you to remember that. But you are groggy with a lifetime of sleep in the all-pervasive conditioning of duality and dualism. So when Ramesh Balsekar wrote his little book that reminded me that Consciousness is all there is and I Am That, I suddenly knew, remembered, and woke up. The deliverance that comes after the wake-up call, which flowed from my own inner voice of wisdom, filled in the details as to how this intuitive knowing that I Am That applies to daily life. It basically meant embracing every detail of life as an extension of that Consciousness that is all there is, as what is—as is. And this meant that everything was exactly as it should be. So there was nothing left to do but *just be*.

It all sounds too simple to be true, but I assure you that if Destiny and Grace have determined that this is the moment for you to cross over that bridge from being the doer in life to just being, all of your onion-vision conditioning will fall away and you will live the rest of the journey with the clarity, freedom, and joy of Pearl Vision.

There is nothing a teacher can add to your being, because you are already perfect as Consciousness. I do see a role for a teacher in the Eastern mystic tradition of "neti-neti." That means "not this—not that." In other words, in your daily Satsang (discourse of truth in holy company) with your teacher, he/she may point out what doesn't fit or is irrelevant to awakening. It is a long process, because practically everything you have ever learned in life about God is either deceptive or irrelevant. But once you have awakened, there is no better teacher than the inner voice of Source speaking directly to you without intermediaries.

So Pearl Vision sees only the need for an awakened person to tell those who are interested enough to seek out the truth that Consciousness is all there is and no individual is a doer separate from Source. The only credential necessary for a teacher is the obvious rapture shining forth that deliverance has produced. If you ask an awakened being what to do to make this happen, you are out of luck! There is nothing anyone can do! There is only one condition necessary for awakening, and that is Destiny and Grace combined to knock your lights out some day with the realization that what your teacher told you is now true for you, too.

My intuition tells me that you seekers are about to have a new wave of awakened beings to hang out and dance with soon. This exchange should not only be fun for you, but also relevant. If you can validate that this is a truly free and happy individual who embraces what is – as is, then when you hear him/her tell you who you are, you may tend to believe it with more credibility than if you only read it in a book. But remember that the teacher/awakened one is no different from you in any way except it was his/her destiny to wake up before you, and before the final curtain call. After that curtain call of death, it is the same return to beingness for all in appearance. Maybe you'll wake up—maybe not! It doesn't matter! It's all the same at the end of the dream after all.

[1] Guru: Teacher.

[2] Roshi: An enlightened sage. A venerable master.

[3] Koan: A paradox to be meditated upon; used in training Zen monks to abandon dependence on reason and gain enlightenment.

[4] Ashram: Hermitage; religious retreat house..

[5] Satori: A direct insight into the true nature of reality.

[6] Sanyas: The vows of renunciation.

[7] Sanyasin: Someone who has taken sanyas and left all worldly pursuits.

CHAPTER 23

SATSANG

In an earlier chapter on spiritual disciplines, the term *Satsang* was mentioned. This discipline was one leg of the three-legged stool of spiritual attainment that is so very prevalent in the Eastern traditions. Take away any leg of a three-legged stool and you promptly flop over on your backside. You already know from my new awareness of the importance (or should I say irrelevance) of any and all spiritual disciplines. If they feel good, are fun, relaxing, or playful, then enjoy them fully in themselves. Not for what you hope to get out of them down the road in some form of measured spiritual attainment. That's why I still meditate every day. It provides me with alone, quiet time to just relax back into the very real Presence of Source and purr with contentment the whole time. Another very high and enjoyable experience is the practice of Satsang.

Please note here the vast difference now between "doing" a discipline because it was prescribed, demanded, or expected of you on a daily basis, and doing it as a way to follow your bliss. Checking back with my experience in various ashrams and with guru hopping, I had to get up at some ungodly hour of the early morning for my first meditation of the day, and sit in a painful rigid posture whether I felt like it or not. My response was always the same. I couldn't sit still for 10 minutes without nodding off. If I was in a Zen Buddhist ashram, the roshi would proceed to whack me out of it by hitting me with his long stick on my shoulder. And so I would spend my whole time drifting in and out of a sleepy stupor.

The same expectation was true of Satsang practiced at most ashrams. You were expected to attend and be an active part for several hours of daily Satsang. This must have its Western equivalent in the requirement to attend Mass on Sunday. A typical Satsang was either the guru up front on a flower-bedecked dais speaking his truth, or in his usual absence, whoever was appointed or volunteered to speak his truth. The content matter of Satsang is always spontaneous, though. The big problem of the speakers other than the guru was that they tended to talk along party lines of what was traditional in that community. Not much chance of exploring new ideas or concepts. In retrospect though, it's just as well. I was confused enough as it was!

So now I want to share with you how Satsang, like meditation, has become fun-filled, exciting, and a high definitely higher than any drug-high experience for me, instead of a dreaded spiritual discipline.

Satsang literally means "a discourse of truth" in Sanskrit. It is normally done with others, although since the wake-up call, it can come roaring within continually from Spirit when I am in the choiceless awareness role as a silent witness. I do believe Jesus was referring to Satsang when he said, "When two or more are gathered in my name, there I am in the midst of you." What I believe he was referring to in this scenario is the incredible energy that is available, which amounts to the synergism of 1 plus 1 equals 100 whenever people gather together with open minds to share their truth or experiences. This is why most workshops today break up into smaller units to share whatever is happening at that point of the focus.

So, with an expanded awareness that comes directly from Source, how do I view Satsang these days? Simply as the most delicious part of the newfound freedom in awakening! Let me explain why. Everything that is being shared with you in this story may be just straining and tugging at your logical mind threads of credibility. After all, I am asking you to disregard a whole lifetime of feeling as if you had free will, and instead look to the Source as the only doer. I am inviting you to relax into an attitude of nondoing, after you have been beating the bushes all your life in an intentional effort for results. So here is where the delightful role of Satsang comes in. Satsang can be the bridge between the impossible stuckness of old conditioning and the incredible new freedom of being awake. Do you realize that Satsang is going on right now at this very moment just by your being engaged in reading this work? New doors of possibility have opened for you already. Are you interested in exploring this further? If you are, that is the Grace of Satsang at work. You can know that I would love to be there with you right now in person and share in your feelings as they come gushing out, usually in the form of questions in the beginning.

If several of your friends were there with you in a similar frame of reference, our combined energy would act as a tidal wave of Grace crashing over all of us. I can assure you that many doubts or confusion would begin to clear up in the exchange of energy, not because of any logical explanations, but because of this mysterious, powerful energy we call Grace, for lack of a better term.

Would it be necessary or even better if I were there with you in person for Satsang? I don't believe so! Remember we are all Source, and no one has a lock on the flow of Grace. It is equally present in everyone, everywhere. The only highlight I could bring with me is the viewpoint of someone who has a foot simultaneously in both the third dimension of the human predicament and the fourth dimension of freedom. The view from what I call the fourth includes an expanded understanding of compassion and love. You see, these words are now the same for me. I use them interchangeably. Love in my new vocabulary is akin to the Biblical God in Genesis looking out over what He had created and saying *all is good.*

Compassion, on the other hand, now has none of the elements for me that are prevalent in conventional wisdom, no pity for, or any desire to reach out and make better what I see.

So when I assist at Satsang and look out over all the shining faces present, I feel love and compassion for all. That simply means I experience everyone there as Source in appearance, most of them stuck in the middle of the human predicament, just like you and I are. And in each face and expression I see, all is so good—so well, just as it is—that I couldn't imagine wanting to change anything about anyone. Let destiny unravel itself! And in Satsang you would feel that linkup of compassion and love, because that is how Source encompasses Its projections. You would not so much hear any words I speak as feel my prevailing attitude of nondoing, surrendered to what is—as is, and hopefully the proof of this shines through my eyes and expression as the fire of joy, peace, and above all, freedom.

The material we are exploring here in this book is reaching out to hit you in your intuitive gut of knowing. This is all old, buried memory of what we truly know at our deepest, unspoken levels. So there, I've said it, and it is all here and in the open now. Satsang is your next step in exploring the gap you feel between the concept of nondoing and the practical living of it in everyday life of surrendered nondoing attitude of freedom. You may read this stuff, sort of understand it, share some Satsang about it with your friends after you have digested it, and then, lo and behold, you begin to understand it at a much deeper level that we call *knowing.* Satsang is that potential linkup between intellectual comprehension and true intuitive knowing at your core essence level.

If we ever do have the opportunity to share Satsang together, we'll have a good laugh at the joke of this whole serious endeavor going on all around us of New Age "seeking." In a gathering of "finders" no longer interested in a search, my expression of joy will beam out this general communication to you between the words, and without the interference of an ego personality to filter out the process: Lighten up here—relax— not all is what it seems to be—no need to improve anyone here—all is well and good as is—you are free at last—fear and karma are done and over with—follow your bliss because nothing else matters in the end!

CHAPTER 24

RELATIONSHIPS AND SOULMATES

To some New Agers, a discussion on relationships is more eagerly sought out than one on enlightenment. This is because of our deep conditioning as an onion that says the key to happiness in life is a meaningful and sexually successful relationship with Mr. or Ms. Right. If this is the key to happiness, it soon becomes apparent that very few have got it. Basically, New Agers are a group of very dedicated seekers who emphasize relationships as the first stop on their journey to Nirvana.[1] If they just keep searching, they are going to find that one individual who is perfect as their potential soulmate. This soulmate has the magic potion that fills up all the holes in their auras, from which their life force is leaking out. The standard profile of your soulmate, yet to be found, includes a person who is intelligent, witty, spiritual, romantic, sensual, sexual, sensitive, good looking, and has the one quality most necessary: "Someone who appreciates you for who you are!"

Well, Pearl Vision has a view on relationships similar to one printed on a T-shirt I bought my wife many years ago: "A woman without a man is like a fish without a bicycle!" In the human predicament, it seems that Source has planted this romantic ideal of relationship into the deepest realms of our conditioning as a surefire way to keep limitation alive and well forever. The core of the human predicament is that we feel separated from God, whatever that means. There's often this annoying, gnawing feeling that somehow we got separated from who we really are and are trapped in separation forever. We don't know how to get back! We don't know exactly what we are separated from, but we know we feel incomplete as we are. Something or someone is missing. Then that sly snake of conditioning comes slithering along and whispers in our ear around puberty, when all the hormones are flowing hot and heavy at full force: "What you need in your life is someone of the opposite sex!" And then our love life becomes automatic chaos from that point on. We even have a myth floating around that, at the moment of our creation, we went from a whole, androgynous being to one that got split in half, one half male, the other female, and the missing half is called our twin flame. So now we spend the rest of our lives looking for not only our own illusory self, but also the illusion of some other part of us in the opposite sex that is our other half and without which we are incomplete and unhappy.

Pearl Vision understands the dilemma of onion vision here. Due to a Divine design factor, mind you, not a design flaw, we come onto this planet believing that we are born separate from the energy that created us. We believe we are independent, autonomous beings with free will and totally in charge of our lives. But we also feel this deep split in the core of our makeup, and we can't for the life of us figure out what is missing. From puberty, on we assume, along with our assumption of self-determination, that what is missing must be located in someone or something outside of ourselves.

Thus begins the search for the twin flame for those who are spiritually sophisticated, soulmates for the New Agers, and Mr. or Ms. Right for the average seeker. This is akin to the search for the pot of gold at the end of the rainbow and has about the same chance of success. Even if you could draw up a profile of exactly what it is you wanted in your relationship, down to the most minute details, and somehow that was given to you, you would not feel the split in your core essence healed. You would instead have to continue your search for something else, like more money or enlightenment, or maybe political power would be the answer.

Do you see how clever this Source is? We have such an itch built into us by conditioning that no amount of scratching can ever satisfy it, thus guaranteeing a lifetime of constant feedback of limitation. Of course, Source also has seen to it that this limitation is balanced evenly by freedom, and so the quest for the unattainable goes on, lubricated by the Freedom/Limitation equation.

Before the wake-up call, I had run the gamut of all possible outlets that might satisfy this mysterious yearning to heal the split. Relationship was always high on my list of possible solutions, and no one ever tried harder than I, neither in quantity nor quality, to check out the perfect soulmate. I was one of those overachievers who had most of what you could want in life at the same time: a loving wife, beautiful daughter, more money than God and the power that goes with it, my own airplane and yachts, perfect health, and homes in the most beautiful countries in the world. But it wasn't enough! Not even close! The itch got worse, but where could I go from there? Nothing left to seek out besides enlightenment, and I had already decided that wasn't a possibility after a futile 40-year quest. I remember the last straw of a solution I reached for in my final despair of "Is this all there is?" I had put a deposit down on a new Citation II jet plane so I could fly higher, faster, and further. One month later, I was arrested for my MDMA activities, definitely a new fork in the road.

In speaking to you about relationship with a soulmate, I come as one who was deeply affected by all the fantasies surrounding this mystique. I have drunk to satiation at the spring of romantic love and grieved its inevitable departure. I have engaged in tantra practices to sexually strengthen the bonds of relationship. I have bared my soul to every type of marriage counselor to try to hang on to a relationship that was slipping away. I have mourned the loss of a soulmate gone off with another lover. I have awakened 10 thousand mornings with the knowledge that my perfect soulmate was out there somewhere, and with new determination and hope of finally finding her. Only at the death of my ego self in that dark cell, in that dark night of the soul, did I realize that romantic love and soulmate relationships were illusions of a separated "me."

But all was not lost in this relationship story! As Pearl Vision gradually replaced onion vision about relationship, what was dead and buried began to come back to life again. The split of separation was healed and it had nothing to do with relationships. I began waking up every morning feeling completely surrounded and permeated by the sweet, gentle Presence of Source. There is so much love, freedom, and safety experienced that I am filled up and overflowing now. And that is the magic word to understand about relationship success— *overflowing.* When you live in the separated mode of "me," you are like an empty sieve in relationships. No matter how much love and appreciation your soulmate pours into you, it is never enough. It just keeps leaking out of all the holes. And then you get angry and disappointed with your lover for his/her inability to forever totally satisfy your needs. When you reconnect with who you really are, the "me" dissolves like disappearing ink and only the "I," as in "I Am That" is present. Words just can't describe that feeling of fullness and freedom one lives with in the Presence of "I Am." Even within the prison walls, the honeymoon with Source is perpetual and complete.

So relationship, as understood and pursued before awakening, is irrelevant now. It has slipped from priority number one to out of sight. A new vision of relationship has emerged, the one of Pearl Vision. When you are filled to overflowing with the sweetness of Presence, nothing more is needed or sought after. However, should destiny place you alongside another mind/body organism that is also filled up and overflowing, then there is no limit to the range of togetherness you can explore. Before awakening, one plus one always equaled two, as in two separate beings crashing into each other. But in the wake of deliverance and subsequent rapture, Oneness is the predominant sensation, no matter how many are around you.

One awakened being plus another awakened being can equal the synergy of a situation you always wanted, but could never achieve in the isolation of only "me" present.

When you don't require anything more of life other than embracing what is—as is, being in what I now call the "sacred relationship" is an outlet for all your overflowing joy, freedom, and love to merge and play with another like-entity. You know better than ever to seek out such a sacred relationship, but when it drops in your lap, well, you know how to appreciate it. When you are searching for a relationship, please understand that you may be doomed to failure in what you really expect from it. When a sacred relationship happens after your awakening, words cannot describe the Oneness that is the core bond of your union and playfulness together.

Relationships can no longer be a two-way street where both individuals are going half way to meet each other in the middle. That's an ideal, however unlikely. A sacred relationship is one plus one merging first into the Oneness, then continuing together in their own unique experience of that Oneness. Yet they are at the same time superimposed without impinging on each other's freedom, because the only freedom felt is that of the Oneness.

When we are in a relationship in the third dimension, we require a very particular and very special significant other. And even if we find such a person, this is almost always a honeymoon of short duration, and soon that special other is now looking oh, so average or even worse. Why? Because initially on meeting that person, we fell in love with the pure energy of Source as Oneness coming through him/her, even if we didn't recognize it as such. But we attributed that loving energy of Source to the other instead of recognizing it for what it was. And so separation into the other is accentuated rather than the Oneness of Source. The relationship is now doomed to either boredom, conflict, or both.

Now enter the fourth dimension where Source is seen in the appearance of all others. Once you have made the shift and know who you are, you naturally know who everyone else is and love everyone more than a third-dimensional person could ever love any one special mate. In the fourth, you are not depending on the other for your love. Love, joy, and freedom flow out of your rapture with life as Source in appearance. Now you can talk about a sacred relationship where the energy field is totally transformed into the playing fields of the Gods. You can look into your soulmate's eyes and see only the dance of Source beckoning you to join in. There is no longer a sense of relating to the other. You are looking at a reflection now of yourself, as Source, as your partner in a sacred relationship. You left judging and comparing behind in the third dimension, so what is left is embracing your partner in whatever behavior dances forth, no matter how outrageous it may turn out to be.

When I first hung out with Rajneesh, he used to tell us that there are two paths to enlightenment: the solitary path of meditation and alone time, and the path of togetherness through a soulmate relationship. Given this choice, you can understand why there was so much free love taking place in the community. Any one of these sanyasins might be that soulmate connection straight through to sudden enlightenment, so we had better try all of them to find the right one! Then right before he died, Rajneesh made a confession to us that he had lied about the soulmate option. He said that if he told us at the beginning that the solitary path was really the only option, no one would take him seriously. So after 20 years of experimentation, and no one reaching enlightenment, when he tells us that relationship is futile in the search for God, maybe now we'll believe him.

One last passing thought to the wise here about awakening and relationships. I can't seem to find any documentation about people starting any new male/female relationships after their awakening. I find plenty of stories about people who received the wake-up call and then continued to spend the rest of their lives with the spouse they were married to before the awakening. And it also seems that in these cases, the spouse never acknowledges the awakening of the husband (sorry, they were all stories about men), even though all his students revered him as a saint. Do you think that is what the Bible meant when it says "No man is a prophet in his own country." Maybe the deliverance is too gradual to be noticed by someone you have already been married to for 25 years. Maybe we like our sages to be more dignified than someone who still belches and farts and can't balance a checkbook. Anyway, I think it speaks volumes for the rapture that a new soulmate relationship never seems to be an issue after the Oneness of Source is experienced.

[1] Nirvana: A state of perfect peace, joy and freedom. The supreme happiness that, according to Buddhism, comes when all passion, hatred, and delusion die out and the soul is released from the necessity of further purification.

HARMLESSNESS

When we hear of Buddha's awakening, the emphasis seems to be on his experience of compassion as the central theme, and his whole teaching afterward seems to reinforce this initial point. Some describe their awakening only in terms of bliss, while others can only talk about love. I would have to relate that, for me, the most predominant experience was of freedom and safety. Maybe being in a maximum security prison, where violence is a way of life, had something to do with this. I don't know. It was like a 1,000-pound sandbag had been lifted off my chest and I felt free from the conditioning of all misinformation.

With Consciousness as the only reality, and the "me" gone as a doer, for the first time I felt safety from those shadows of imminent doom and from that something critical I had to do but never knew what it was. Yes, there was a kind of love present—the love of seeing the appearance of the whole creation for the first time as Source sees and embraces all that is good (my only definition of love = embracing what is–as is). There was some compassion of the Source, looking out over the appearance and experiencing the human predicament It had created, knowing It had a built-in safety factor. Of course, there is sometimes bliss, and always the peace of the rapture, where not only all is well, but you also want to celebrate it by dancing on the ceiling. Also present in the rapture is a constant, nonstop awareness of Source as a felt Presence.

But if we have to pick the predominant feeling that awakening triggered for me, its name is FREEDOM.

After talking about how people experience their wake-up calls, there is one common denominator that runs through everyone's deliverance, no matter what his/her background. Harmlessness is a central function of the deliverance. Once you realize that Consciousness permeates all that is, and there are no free agents running around this universe who are not Pure Consciousness, a tremendous respect and reverence takes over your awareness in dealing with the rest of the world. Here's where that Sanskrit phrase "Namaste" becomes your constant mantra as each person, plant, animal, and event touches your senses.

In the human predicament we have all inherited, whether we realize how deeply it runs or not, there is an enormous amount of resistance to what is—especially the *As Is* part. We spend most of our lives wishing to change *As Is* into a "me" version of it. As part of harmlessness, this resistance melts into a state of sweet surrender to every detail of what is—as is. It sees only the Oneness of Source in every act of the Leela, in every actor within the Leela, and in all the various stage props used by the Leela. How can you cause harm, whether bodily, emotionally, or even in thought, to yourself or others when you intuitively know you are only dealing with Source?

It looks like Francis of Assisi embodied this spirit of harmlessness as it flowed out of his surrender throughout his life after his awakening. This was in great contrast to his former life as a warrior.

Harmlessness and surrender cannot be sought out as desirable traits to be acquired. They just happen naturally as the deliverance gradually clears up the muddy waters of conditioning. When you experience this reverence for life and see atrocities of cruelty being perpetrated, you can see the perfection of Source in appearance, in action, in limitation. Not something for you to fix, or make better, or even understand. Just the sweet freedom of allowing whatever is to remain exactly as it is because you are seeing through the Maya and keeping your focus on the Director of this Leela. And while

CHAPTER 25

harmlessness cannot be obtained through the intentional effort of a discipline, it will always be present as the honey that flows out of the deliverance.

CHAPTER 26

DRUGS

Right behind the interest in relationship issues comes the fascination for drugs out of the "baby boomer" generation. This interest can be attributed to our inherited human predicament. Drugs have always been around, but mostly the kind that help to take you out of the human predicament for a short while. In this last generation, we have been exposed to uppers like cocaine and speed that accentuate the activity of the mind. But we have also seen new mind-expanding drugs like LSD, mood enhancers like Ecstasy, and the spiritual appeal for psilocybin in magic mushrooms.

At the core of our human predicament lies the tremendous feeling of alienation from our true Self as Source. The small separated self of ego, nurtured by a lifetime of conditioning, feels like it is on its own autonomous path through this scary world of cruel and ruthless practices. Anything that can temporarily alleviate that panic of separation, even for a little while, is held in esteem regardless of the consequences. For as long as we have recorded history, we have a record of prostitution, drugs, alcohol, and gambling. And for just as long a period, we can follow the law of the land trying to legislate the morality of these escapes from reality (human predicament). And for the same period they have never succeeded, nor will this current war on drugs ever work, until the split in man's human predicament is healed completely. And don't hold your breath waiting!

What is interesting here, however, is the current universal interest in psychotropic drugs, drugs that expand the mind in an attempt to understand our reality from a more spiritual approach, instead of just escaping into the anesthesia of a numbed awareness. Awareness seems to be enhanced here as we probe for answers to the mysteries of the human predicament. A common reaction to these drug experiences is the absence of fear about living on the planet and a unique feeling of oneness with all of nature. There is a delight in the simple side of life, as opposed to the complexities of the rat race. But somehow, these temporary insights and feelings do not carry over to our daily lives in the marketplace after the drug has worn off. So we try them again next weekend. Maybe they will work longer this time!

There is no drug available on this planet that can permanently open your eyes to who you really are. The most they can usually do, under ideal circumstances, is open that door of perception for a moment, and then slam it shut in your face. That really accentuates the limitation. Now you have tasted a tidbit of the enormous joy that awareness can bring, and then been turned away from the banquet table hungry and empty handed. If you could permanently stay high on a mind-expanding drug trip, you might like it better than facing reality sober, but all drugs have a built-in safety factor—tolerance. Sooner or later, the drug doesn't work unless you increase its amount and frequency. Sooner or later, you crash and burn out.

I speak out here as living proof and testimony that the cheap and easy thrill I got out of searching for meaning out of psychedelics and psychotropics is like a grain of sand on the beach of awareness that comes from knowing who you are. Now that the experience of consciousness being all there is remains as present as my breath, it is unimaginable to seek any relief from the human predicament or any answers to questions that dried up long ago in my deliverance through drugs.

If there was a drug that could wake you up in either one trip or a thousand trips, I would say, "Go for it!" Such a drug would have to enable you to know and feel fully what I have been saying all along here. Such a drug would have to keep the knowing going strong, even in the face of extreme situations of the human predicament. Such a drug would have to never wear off, even in the dreams of sleep. Unfortunately for the human predicament, there isn't such a drug!

I've had inmates come to me and ask me why they are so addicted to heroin or crack cocaine. My only response is that obviously the Source is wanting to have an experience of limitation that drug abuse provides so well, but not to mentally beat themselves up for it or lower their self-esteem afterwards. If you understand that you are not the doer and become the silent witness who monitors what happens without judgment or preference, addiction has a way of falling away by itself in time. Intentional effort is not the answer, as we can see by the 90 percent recidivism back into drug use through conventional treatment. But when awareness of Source enters the picture, your head is already in the mouth of the tiger and there is no escaping. Why is it that a person will have to dry out 87 times in a futile effort to beat his habit and then one day, it just mysteriously falls away? Grace, timing, and destiny are at work here! Drug counselors don't want to hear this kind of explanation, but how can I say otherwise? If I could put the experience of a wake-up call, with the clarity of the deliverance and joy of the rapture that all come together into a pill form and dispense it, I would have the whole human population as steady customers. And if Source wanted the whole human race to taste of this experience, it could be done in a microsecond with a Divine thought energy transfer. What is, is the human predicament—as is! In an attempt to change that, man will always resort to drugs in one form or another, however futile the long-term results. So it seems that drugs are here to stay as part of our Freedom/Limitation role in the Divine Leela.

CHAPTER 27

BODHISATTVAS

This is an ancient Buddhist term for those souls who have taken a perpetual vow that they will not leave the Earth plane as enlightened until every other soul in the universe has been enlightened, as a practice of compassion. In the meantime, they are just supposed to reincarnate over and over as God's little helpers and struggle on in the darkness, until the job is complete. I'm sure God is grateful for their help and compassion!

This fits in nicely with the story I hear all the time from the New Agers, repeating that they all are souls who "volunteered" in a courageous manner to leave the bosom of the Father and come to the planet on a special mission. Part of the mission includes a veil of forgetfulness, so that their true origins and the nature of their mission would be forgotten. They even claim that they picked out their parents, children, and family by mutual consent at some heavenly weekend flea market as the first step in undertaking the mission. Those that could afford it probably used a universal computer service to match up potential parents and soulmates for their mission.

There is one more New Age group we ought to include here. That is the equally outrageous story of these 144,000 ascended masters who have lived various earthly lives, achieved enlightenment, ascended then as perfect masters, and now keep coming back to aid the planet in her spiritual evolution. However, they are subject to that same veil of forgetfulness and when they are wandering around earth, they are just as lost as everyone else, that is, until they receive the trumpet call to put on their armor, sharpen their old swords, remember who they are, and head for the prearranged battle stations. How do you know if you are one of these 144,000 chosen souls? Simple: If you think you might be one, or would like to be one, then you qualify. You are one!

You know, it never ceases to amaze me how many "chosen people" of God are running around the planet, starting with the old tribes of Israel, blending into the elite of Catholicism, and down to these present-day ascended masters. Let's get back to the drawing board here, folks. There are no favorite sons, tribes, Bodhisattvas, religions, scriptures, or chosen people of God! Never have been—never will be! What we are dealing with in the basics of Pearl Vision is that THERE IS ONLY CONSCIOUSNESS—nothing else! Consciousness can take any infinite number of forms, but it is still One Consciousness—equally and fully in every single individual form. As part of Its Leela to amuse Itself, when It comes into manifestation in the world of phenomenon, It can pretend It is any and all combinations of Limitation—the more the merrier. The more real It looks and feels, the more enjoyable the Leela becomes. Why not pretend you are a Bodhisattva or an ascended master, or maybe just a plain old brave soul who volunteered to leave the heavenly bliss to come to this low-density vibrational mass? Great casting! It certainly balances off all the millions of demons and devils that the Christian fundamentalists focus their energy on.

Another very common story that circulates in New Age circles leads to the conclusion that when you are experiencing some particular trouble in the human predicament, God is testing you, or that this is a new lesson, or maybe it is to strengthen your resolve and your will power. Friends, Source does not need any lessons or testing. It already knows it all! This is a dream about limitation. The dream is scheduled to end. No time has actually elapsed. No damage has been done. No lessons learned. Nobody died, because they were never born!

One of the most delightful sensations of the rapture comes from the viewing of absolute reality against the backdrop of all old, previous conditioning. For the first few months, you are almost dysfunctional from laughing so hard. After a while, you acclimate to the constant "joke" that is happening all around you at every moment and manage to get by with wearing a mischievous smile, sort of like the cat who swallowed the canary. I stress again, the use of "Namaste" comes easily to one's lips when confronted with so many different ideas floating around, of souls separate from God, with their freedom of choice in choosing missions in various lives, past, present, and future. This kind of disinformation is certainly useful in perpetuating the myths that cause such juicy limitation for Source in appearance. And thus the Leela continues—alive and well!

CHAPTER 28

PREDISPOSITIONS

One of the many marvels of Pearl Vision is seeing, enjoying, and gasping in awe at the way the One displays Its appearance in the diversity of the many. Each and every time that Source leaves resting in Its Being and comes into appearance, the manifestation is unique from all others. Source does not want to get bored by the same old, same old. It comes into the appearance of an individual mind/body organism to effect some unique circumstances It has in mind. So an absolutely unique individual with certain "predispositions" becomes another bubble on the surface of the fabric of being.

Modern psychology is picking up where ancient science, like astrology, left off about the nature of people's unique personality traits. Rather than go through all these studies of human categories with you, I will only mention the one that has impressed me the most, and that is the Enneagram. This system was developed thousands of years ago, then promulgated by the Sufis, and now is the darling of modern approaches to predicting behavioral outcome by knowing one's number and wing within the Enneagram system. It is surprisingly accurate on details. I do believe that when we get more sophisticated in the knowledge and workings of DNA, we will find everyone's unique predispositions of character and personality already preset into the DNA strand at the moment of conception. So much for my views of nature versus nurture theories!

How these predispositions get here isn't as important as is their function. Source comes into appearance as an individual mind/body organism to have a unique experience of diversity and limitation. How diversity/limitation plays out is determined by the predispositions infused and balanced by the Freedom/Limitation equation. The drama ensues from the moment of conception onwards. Whether this particular bag of skin reaches any degree of awakening or not, one factor remains constant—the predispositions. That is why we find awakened masters who were impatient and irascible before awakening and the very same way afterwards. The same for the gentle, nurturing masters we see caring for people. Those qualities were basically already in their inherited predispositions before they ever received their wake-up call.

An example of predisposition is in order here. Before my wake-up call I was, according to the Enneagram, a seven with an eight wing. Someone familiar with the Enneagram system would now be able to describe about 90 percent of my various characteristics, how I view the world, and my normal reactions in the survival process. Then came the awakening. I am still a seven with an eight wing. That part of my personality is my predisposition. Even though the ego personality dissolves in the shift, how it was set up to operate is still functioning in pretty much the same way. I may only be 80 percent predictable now by an Enneagram specialist, but basically this set of predispositions is not going to radically change just because I did. After all, Source loves the diversity and uniqueness in each of us. It went to a lot of trouble to make sure that each and every one of us is different. What a bummer for Source if the shift to the fourth dimension makes us all little clones. No, that percentage of me that is not predictable as a seven with an eight wing goes outside of my predispositions and makes me absolutely unique in the diversity of this universe.

Awakening means you suddenly see clearly, know intuitively, and feel completely that all there is, is Consciousness and as a result of that breakthrough, that the ego as "me" is not the doer. There is only Source acting through the individual mind/body organism. So Source plays each role differently when there is a wake-up call programmed for an individual. In one scenario, it becomes a teacher and beats the ignorance out of the student with a stick. In another, it is kind and gentle and sensitive to the confusion of the student. In a third, it says, "To hell with teaching ignorant onions, I'm going off by myself and enjoy the rapture of this Pearl Vision without having to deal with any more stupid questions." Hey, it happens!

There is no format set in stone as to how an individual mind/body organism is supposed to act, or be, or do, upon awakening. Each one is different and one-of-a-kind, although there are some common areas of deliverance. What determines how one acts after awakening is the same as what determines how one acts before awakening, namely, your predispositions. Awakened ones who play the role of a great teacher stirring the masses out of their apparent lethargy may end up being persecuted or even killed, because those playing the roles of onions don't like anyone disturbing their nice, neat layers of conditioning—not even a shiny Pearl!

That old Zen adage about what you did before you were enlightened—chop wood and carry water, and what you did after enlightenment—chop wood and carry water, is true only for the survivalists. It means that there is no need to make any drastic changes in your lifestyle, career, or relationship once you wake up. Your inherited predispositions will determine how you live out the rest of your life, and they don't change with awakening. What you see is what you get! But not all is as it seems!

CHAPTER 29

AVATARS

By avatars,[1] I mean the biggies of the awakened ones in history, like Lao Tzu, Buddha, Jesus, Mohammed, and Krishna. It is not that their awakening was bigger than most, because awake is awake. There are no degrees of awake, only degrees of deliverance and rapture. It's not that they were special to Source, because Source doesn't have any favorite sons. How can It when there is only One and the same energy radiating out from formless potential to form? In no individual appearance is there any more or less of Source present. So what makes them the biggies that stand out? They had leading roles in the drama of their days.

They wore a unique and different mask for each act of the play. They came along at that point in the unfolding of the big Dream where Source wanted to run a different course of events, so It showed up as an avatar to be the catalyst in the ensuing world changes. Take Jesus for example. Through this avatar's influence of teaching and demonstrating God's love to mankind, we got Christianity, and you know what that means to Source. How many millions of people have slaughtered each other in the name of that God, Jesus, and Christianity over the last 2,000 years? If that isn't an experience of limitation, then what is?

Look at Buddha. He had a remarkable experience of waking up after seeking enlightenment for years through unbelievable austerities. He sat under the Bodhi tree for a couple of weeks integrating his deliverance and enjoying his rapture. Then he spent the next 40 years of his life teaching and writing

10,000 (literally 10,000, I kid you not) rules and regulations about how to live, what to do and not do, to emulate this experience of Oneness with Source that was his wake-up call.

Don't you just love the cosmic joke taking place when Lord Krishna counsels his disciple Arjuna to go kill all his cousins and their friends in the big battle coming up because it was his destiny?

> As a result of Krishna, we have Hinduism.
> As a result of Jesus, we have Christianity.
> As a result of Buddha, we have Buddhism.
> As a result of Mohammed, we have Islam.
> As a result of Lao Tzu, we have Taoism.

The only ones not slaughtering each other in the name of their founding avatars, are the Taoists, and that's because there are too few of them left in China to be a warrior influence.

Lao Tzu's wisdom became a legend in his own time and so he was appointed Court Director of Metaphysics. He got bored with the impenetrable ignorance of his students and escaped one night on the back of a water buffalo. But they caught up with him and held him hostage until he wrote out his entire wisdom and the understanding of his deliverance. So he knocks out 81 teeny, tiny, poetic verses overnight that he called *Tao Te Ching*, meaning "the way of no path," and they let him go. To me, this is the only scripture that makes perfect sense, but you have to be awake to even understand it. I had read it for many years before and loved the sound of it. But only after the wake-up call did I begin to understand it.

Avatars were worshiped by their followers and the subsequent descendants of their followers, who by then had formed official religions. The description of the teachings of the avatars developed into well-known scriptures and bibles. But as we well know, religion and scriptures are the toughest layer of conditioning and limitation to break through and finally discard in our movement toward awakening, at least the dogmatic, stuck parts that tend to limit our freedom. So along with the freedom of their teachings and the examples of love and compassion, we really got a healthy dose of limitation in the subsequent religions and scriptures that were also part of their equation.

The last thing that any avatar could have wanted was to be worshiped down the line. They were most likely not born fully awakened. The wake-up call came later. They were so extraordinary in the ordinary way they lived their lives. And yes, they were part of the human predicament the same as anyone else. Their lives showed the very same balance of the Freedom/Limitation equation. They were the greatest proof that Source manifests equally in human appearance; some awaken, some don't, but it's all the same life experience when it all balances out overall.

There were some few reported miracles in the case of Jesus, but by and large, Source prefers to live out the human predicament without the copious use of miracles. Miracles are on the freedom side of the balance and would require a lot of limitation to balance them. Look at all the miracles of Jesus and then the way he ended up on a cross at the end. Balance! Source does not come into appearance to experience only freedom. That's already a given of Source at rest. What It is playing with is limitation in the human predicament, avatar or not!

If we distill the wisdom of the avatars down to a simple message, it is the oneness of all things, so we end up where we started: Consciousness is all there is. Yet out of this simple message and four avatars: Jesus, Krishna, Mohammed, and Buddha, we have 98 percent of the planet's religious diversity pretending that theirs is the only approach to God, and that is to die for! So the main message of the avatar, which is pure freedom, has spawned the greatest source of all conflict, which is limitation, and that keeps the human predicament stewing in its own juices. The avatars showed us the way home to freedom and expansion. But so far, humanity prefers to engage in limitation and contraction instead, along the way of our lawful unfolding.

I have an insight I would like to share with you. Even

though we have had some pretty amazing avatars throughout human history, their personal impact was not enough to shift all the seekers into finders. But they did prepare general consciousness for the big shift. I believe that shift is now occurring. I don't think any more avatars are necessary for this shift into the fourth dimension because it is happening at a personal inner level for all seekers, no matter what culture or religion they come from. Source is getting ready to play Consciousness with new rules of engagement that don't necessitate any more avatars. The new rules are simple:

> Know that Consciousness is all there is.
> Know that you are not the doer.
> Know that you don't have to win awakening by
> your efforts.
> Just be and know WHO you really are.
> Then kick back and enjoy the parade as it passes by!

---

[1] Avatars: Divine incarnations.

CHAPTER 30

LOVE
AND
FEAR

Part of our human predicament is having to deal with the inevitable duality that the use of our intellect creates. As we see, feel, and sense objects, the mind automatically breaks everything down into the polarity of duality. This wouldn't be so constrictive if we did it as silent witnesses in choiceless awareness. But that's not the human *modus operandi*. We instinctively make judgments about each entry we receive, and that moves simple duality into dualism, choosing one side of the polarity over the other.

For example, I see Dr. Jack Kevorkian on the TV news. On seeing his image my mind evokes the concept of euthanasia. The duality occurs here when that assisted suicide is either an act of compassion or morally wrong—right or wrong! Then depending on my preconditioning, my mind makes a judgment and forms an opinion or preference for one side over the other. That is dualism. Love and fear are two sides of a polarity.

Love is one side of duality or polarity as a possible outcome. Love is on the freedom side of the Freedom/Limitation balance. Love is what we are naturally as Source at rest. We don't have to learn how to love because that's who we are by essence. Now, the other side of the love coin is not hate, but fear. Hate is but one of the many attributes of fear. Fear is on the limitation side of the balance. Fear is the head of all "negative" emotions, just as love is the head of all "positive" emotions. So there are really only two emotions, love and fear, from which all other human emotions spring. Fear is not natural to us as

Source. We have to learn fear as we learn about and experience limitation through our conditioning.

When I speak of love, I don't mean the romantic version of the illness that afflicts us as teenagers when we say, "I'm in love." I use love as the only way I know, as Source looked out over all It had created and according to Genesis, It said, "All is good!" That is love! That embracing of all that is, as is, as good, as an emanation from the Source.

Fear, on the other hand, is a resistance to what is—as is. So we could say:

$$\left.\begin{array}{l} \text{Love = Surrender} \\ \text{Fear = Resistance} \end{array}\right\rangle \text{ to What Is—As Is}$$

This understanding is the heart of the deliverance factor I keep mentioning. The awakening is the understanding of the reality that Consciousness is all there is, and that we are not the doers. But the deliverance is the flow of ramifications from this understanding that is then lived every moment of every day. That's why we understand that love is the process of surrendering your life to all that you experience, as Source in appearance, in a way that accepts, allows, and embraces each event, without judging it as negative, without an opinion about it, without even an attitude of preference one way or the other. This is love in freedom!

Fear flips this whole state over to a process of resisting events in your life as negative, as unwanted, as something to change, to fix, or to make go away. Fear/resistance maintains a critical, complaining, fault-finding attitude about undesirable events in life, instead of seeing the hand, energy, and wisdom of Source at play. This is fear in limitation! But because fear/resistance is a learned conditioning, it can be unlearned when the deliverance strips these layers away.

I can remember a good friend of mine, Stuart Wilde, who had amazing insights into the world of Spirit, giving me one of these jewels of wisdom once. This happened about a year before my arrest, when we were in Las Vegas playing Blackjack all night long. He sat me down and, although it seemed quite incongruous for the time and place, told me that the greatest obstacle to my awakening was my overall resistance to life. He did not elaborate greatly on this, and I did not understand what he meant. But I never forgot it, because it was one of those lightening bolts of truth that hit you every so often. Then, when I was arrested and consulted with a couple of well-known spiritual psychic channelers for any information they could give me about my legal status, they both casually mentioned my "anti" attitude of resistance that was somehow involved in this whole mess. That wasn't what I was asking for, but there it was again!

Only after about a year of deliverance after the wake-up call did I really, deeply understand what Stuart and the psychics meant about resistance. And probably that's why they didn't go into any lengthy explanations of it. Without the clarity of the wake-up call, it would be unintelligible, because fear/resistance is too deeply ingrained in us from our earliest conditioning.

I keep pointing out how clever Source is in this game of Freedom/Limitation. Who could have imagined that the point of the greatest, most severe limitation in my life—a maximum security prison term—was also the point of the greatest liberation from conditioning, or freedom, at the same time. Before prison, in my seeking for Source, I somehow intuitively imagined that Spirit was to be found in the quiet beauty of Nature. So acting on this many years ago, I bought a mountaintop in Costa Rica that was a mile high, had the most incredible views, and the world's greatest climate. No money was spared to develop the property into a huge Zen garden with fountains, waterfalls, and winding paths. Here I could do my zazen up on a platform over the water tower at sunrise and sunset, and reflect on Spirit during my walking meditations through the gardens. Perfect setup for awakening, right? Not so! It only served to deepen my feelings of alienation from this whole human predicament. How did I end up on the wrong planet like this? I felt like a stranger in a strange land.

Now let's quickly change the scenery for the next act of Source's stage play. We switch to a hot, filthy, crowded, underground dungeon of a county jail where I lived for two years. The opposite of everything I experienced in my home-monastery in Costa Rica. But it's here that the wake-up call came! Then we shift again out to a federal maximum security prison at Terminal Island. Here the deliverance commences. All day—every day—100 times a day, I am confronted with situations of extreme limitation. Violence, hatred, hostility, oppression, bullies, rapes, riots, solitary confinement in the hole[1]— need I go on? There is never a respite from physical and psychological limitation in prison life. But what has happened here is the gradual day-by-day seeing of the hand of Source in all of this. The melting away of resistance into surrender. The changeover of fear into the embrace of love.

At first, I was elated at my sentencing when the Judge saw fit to recommend that I be sent to the nicest prison camp in their system, Nellis Air Force Base in Las Vegas. But instead, the Bureau of Prisons sent me to their worst, most over-crowded, most gang-banger infested prison with gun-tower security. After my initial panic, I began to realize that there was more to this than meets the eye. Nellis couldn't begin to compare to Terminal Island for offering the extreme conditions of limitation that apparently were necessary to shine the clear light of deliverance onto the human predicament. It looks now, in retrospect, that trying to get through the maze of deliverance in a situation such as meditating in my monastery in Costa Rica would have been operating in a vacuum. You don't learn about surrender unless there is a strong potential resistance to push against you along the way. Remember Nietzsche saying "That which doesn't kill me, makes me stronger?" Well, the complement to that statement is: "That fear, which I yield to as Source in play, gives me an experience of love in the end."

More fear yielding to more love.
More limitation yielding to more freedom.
More resistance yielding to more surrender.

---

[1] Hole: A nasty place in which the guards house inmates in solitary confinement.

LIFE IN THE FOURTH DIMENSION

CHAPTER 31

THE GREATEST MIRACLE

If we review the course of human history, we find that Source has resorted to the use of miracles very sparingly. By a miracle here, let's just refer to events that are outside the natural course of nature. Some so-called miracles are really following the laws of nature, but we haven't gotten that far in our intellectual understanding of how the universe functions. Jesus, walking on water, would be in the category of a miracle. The stigmata of St. Francis and Lazarus rising from the dead would also fit in here. But instant cures from faith healing may or may not fit until we better understand the function of the mind and attitude in maintaining health.

We may be more able to understand the scarcity of miracles if we can see that Source did not leave the peace of rest to come into a dream appearance to get flooded with little hokey freedoms we call miracles, when It already is the ultimate and infinite source of all freedom in Its makeup as Essence. Pure and simple, Source is here to experience the *ordinary* human predicament of limitation, and miracles momentarily free us from that predicament. A miracle here and there, now and then, may serve nicely to emphasize an apparent contrast or make a point, but we don't find them as a normal part of the human predicament.

Somewhat more common than miracles are parapsychological events. They are not miraculous, and we still can't fully understand how they fit in the scheme of the natural law yet. Mental telepathy—clairvoyance—kinesthesis—levitation—channeling—visions—all fit this category. Someday we may understand these events, and everyone will have access to them. But what I want to emphasize here is that we should not be too impressed with events that happen out of the ordinary or desire them for our own use, not even so-called "spiritual" gifts. If they happen, fine! If not, not to worry! There is normally no connection whatsoever between any miracle or parapsychological power and one's awakening process. They are only like sideshows within the big circus of life, meant more for entertainment than for spiritual significance.

We see millions of Indians following a guru around because he can materialize items out of the air, and missing most likely, any real connection to the spiritual insight that the guru has to offer. They, as Source, prefer the entertainment value here more than getting down to the nitty-gritty, like surrender and the dissolution of ego.

There is only one miracle that I do want to discuss, and that is the greatest miracle of all—one's awakening process. I don't know of one single person to wake up from the multiple miracles Jesus performed. When the sideshow was over, they went home and later crucified him for more entertainment. Those weeping Madonna statues all over the world that are the latest rage now in producing miracles, to my knowledge, haven't produced a single awakened being yet.

In the natural course of events, we are born into the human predicament of multilayered conditioning. We live our whole lives in it and end up dying in it. We may be seekers and add on some extra layers of spiritual conditioning, but that seeking has only strengthened the power of the ego in its quest as a separate entity from that which is sought. No, the real and only miracle to focus on is that miraculous process by which one is transported by Grace out of the clutches of a separated ego personality and back into the perspective and experience of Source.

Just how miraculous is this process? Well, in the *Bhagavad Gita*, Lord Krishna tells Arjuna that the words of wisdom he is relating to him will only be heard by one person in a thousand and of those that hear it, only one in a thousand will really get it. That figures out to one in a million individual mind/body organisms that ever break free from the human predicament to awakening (if you believe Krishna). Maharaj Nasargadatta, an awakened master in India who guided Ramesh Balsekar, a contemporary and to me, the clearest of all sages, is far more conservative. And he should know, for he taught as an awakened one with lots of in-depth field experience for more than 40 years. He says only one in 100 thousand hear this and only one of these 100 thousand who hear it ever realize it. Those odds are more like one in 10 billion. This may be a slight exaggeration on his part for the sake of emphasis, but you see what I mean about the miracle of ever getting out of the human predicament. My personal view is that there are really many, many more awakened ones walking around than meets the eye. But maybe these beings are enjoying the beauty of their Pearl Vision in private, without making a fuss over it, so nobody really knows.

I also feel that these forecasts of Krishna and Nasargadatta were only true for their times. My present awareness is that all around me there is shifting taking place from the third to the fourth dimension, so much so that I can call this shift the New Age of freedom. I don't know of anything like this happening before in the human predicament. More about this "shift" later.

Do you know that in the Zen tradition of awakening, when a monk finally reaches satori, he stays in the monastery for at least 10 more years of integrating this shift, similar to what I am calling the deliverance. Then he is sent out on the road to teach his realizations. However, if he comports himself in such a way that people immediately recognize that here walks an enlightened one, he is too obvious, and so he is sent back to the monastery for a further tune-up. He has to learn how to be just an ordinary man, which is a most extra-ordinary occurrence.

By the very fact that you are reading here the kind of Satsang that Krishna and Nasargadatta were talking about, you are qualified to consider yourself part of that first group who get exposed to nondual Satsang. If these words cause a rush of goose bumps and an intuitive "Ahhhh!" of recognition of the truth, then you can also be part of the second group. Either way, your head is in the mouth of the tiger, and you are not going to escape!

So, what should you do about this awakening process now that your attention has been caught? How do you cash in your universal lottery ticket before death cashes you in? Well, this book is designed to help you relax into not doing anything, but just be and relax any intentional efforts to make the awakening happen. This is all a matter of Destiny and Grace. The moment you were conceived, you had already bought your ticket, and the winning numbers were already posted. So there's nothing you can do about it now anyway, except wait and see what happens.

This attitude should take an enormous load off your head. Once you enter the curse of being a seeker, after the delightful ignorance of being a nonseeker, nothing can satisfy you until you have captured the goal of enlightenment, (or so you think). But you already are enlightened by being Source in appearance, so the next-best goal would be to wake up to who you really are. (In case I forgot to tell you—there are no goals!) You can simply believe me and quit trying to ask any more questions, because every answer just raises two more questions about it. All is well—just as it is! But I can already hear you asking, "Okay, we believe you! So what do we do about it?"

If you are still driven to act on your seeking, at least do it with the awareness that you are not the doer, that Source is playing this game of limitation through you, that you are going to act "as if" you were still the doer, but deep down, you know it's just a front for Source. Relish quiet time alone. That is the cabbage patch from which miracles of transmutation can take place. Now that you understand at least intellectually what we are discussing, this comprehension will percolate down to your intuitive chambers of the heart and then explode from your gut with absolute knowing beyond words, beyond explanation.

While all this is taking place, you can assure the part of you that still harbors doubt and fear about the scary parts of life that

Source is in control here, backed up by infinite wisdom and a game plan that is perfect. You don't get to understand that game plan until you wake up! And then you won't care anymore! When you finally are in a position to have all your answers to life, the questions all dry up. There's only one song playing on that jukebox in your head after awakening: Consciousness is all there is and I Am That! In fact, after a couple of years of deliverance, the song changes to I—I. In other words, you start relating to life as Source without form, instead of Source in appearance as form. This is getting pretty subtle here, so let's leave it at that rather than confuse you with an impossible explanation. In fact, the only explanation will be your own experience.

CHAPTER 32

PREDICTIONS FOR THE PLANET

There are a few magazines floating around, which I used to subscribe to, that are dedicated solely to channeled information that comes from ascended masters like Sananda (the former Jesus in a new lightform body), to little aliens from outer space. The majority of the information deals with the immense changes that are going to take place on the planet as we move into the 21st Century. Most of the channels also advertise their many books written on these subjects to further elucidate their predictions. The predictions are so varied and esoteric that they cancel each other out by contradiction. The majority are presenting a picture of man, as we know him, moving into a light body made of particles or waves, a pure and high consciousness, and totally aware. Man in an ascended form—more angel actually than man. They are presenting a planet free of war, pollution, famine, etc. In other words, the same way we would do it if we were God, as we fantasized in an earlier chapter.

If you read between the lines in all these predictions, no one is satisfied with the planet as it is. To help change everything and make it better for everyone, we are enlisting the help of all the ascended avatars on the spiritual plane and all the aliens for advanced technology on the material plane. Obviously, either Source doesn't know how to create a decent planet, or It has seen the error of Its ways and is now correcting all mistakes in the New Age.

Are you ready for another possibility, one that doesn't see any major changes coming? Why would Source, who is on an insatiable quest for limitation in this world of appearance, suddenly decide to basically eliminate all forms of limitation and substitute unlimited freedom instead? Its experience already is infinite freedom at rest. It only allows enough freedom into the life experience of limitation to keep it tolerable and still enjoyable as a playful dream.

I see every known disaster, disease, and chaotic situation on the planet ending some day, only to be replaced by new and different forms of the same limitation. I see the ratio of awakened Pearls to sleeping onions remaining the very same. If we take all these New Agers and seekers running around, who yearn for vast and higher ranges of aware consciousness, and add them all up, they still don't, and won't, equal even 1 percent of the world's population. These are probably the ones who are moving toward awakening, and that's why they yearn so. They are only receiving the thoughts and impulses from Source. So they reach out through the channelers and prophets to paint a new and glorious picture for this tired old planet. They are sure that there is some magic key or formula that unlocks the secret of universal enlightenment, if only they keep looking and trying and shaking those bushes.

But here is my experience with these seekers, which is also turning into a prediction for the planet. While I don't see the entire planet shifting from the third to the fourth dimension all at once, it does look to me like those 1 percent who are yearning, burning seekers are already starting to shift here and there, now and then, into the fourth dimension. That 1 percent may even grow into a larger percentage as the years go by. But because I don't foresee the whole planet shifting, those who do end up in the fourth dimension will walk with a foot in each dimension, to the great amusement of Source.

One last observation about all these predictions for the planet: In the witnessing of the human predicament, there are two salient features to keep in mind. One, you never really know the future or outcome of anything—by Divine design! Two, you can't do anything about it anyway. Not knowing and powerlessness are powerful tools of Source to keep the game of limitation alive and well. That's why the predictions are out there—to play with you and get your hopes up. Is subsequent disappointment a limitation? You bet it is! So take them all with a grain of salt. No matter how it turns out, it's all the same in the Freedom/Limitation equation anyway!

CHAPTER 33

THE GREAT COSMIC JOKES

You think you have to get enlightened.
You already are.

You think you have to follow a path to get there.
There are no paths.

You think enlightenment is a goal.
There are no goals.

You think you have to change yourself and the world
to make it a better place.
There is nothing to do.

You think you can find God in India or Tibet.
There is nowhere to go. Consciousness is the same everywhere.

You think the outcome of your personal story matters.
It is all the same, regardless of how it turns out.

You think your story is real.
It is an illusion, a dream.

You think you are in control of your life.
You are but a puppet of Source.

You think you have free will and make choices.
There is only destiny in its lawful unfolding.

You think you have enemies out there.
There is only Source out there.

You think there is a magic formula to finding God.
Relax, you are already home in It.

You think everyone's drama is a reality.
It's all done with smoke and mirrors.

You think God wants higher consciousness on the planet.
Source is only here to play in limitation.

You think God holds you responsible.
There is no karma.

You entertain judgments—comparisons—
opinions—preferences.
There is only what is–as is, exactly as it should be.

You want to be somebody important and appreciated.
Just be.

You fear death as the most tragic event of your life.
Death is the end of limitation.

You hope for a better life the next time around.
There is no self to reincarnate. There is only Source as I AM.

You regret the past, worry in the present,
and fear for the future.
You are infinite Source having a playful dream. Relax!

You are intrigued by complex conspiracy theories.
There is only Source amusing Itself.

You think you have a purpose in life.

There is no individual "me" to have a purpose. There is only Source. It does have a purpose for this appearance. You don't get to know that purpose through a finite mind.

CHAPTER 34

TRUTH

Man's quest for truth is exceeded only by his quest for pleasure. There is a part of the human predicament that itches constantly, that is tied into wanting to know the truth about all possible levels of knowledge. Yet no matter how much we scratch it with facts, it doesn't go away. It's always still there! That is because we are only dealing with relative truth if we are using words. Any time you have to think or express a thought, you have to use words. By definition, those words limit the understanding of an idea, either through semantics or limitation of scope. It is with small wonder, then, that our thirst for truth is never quenched. It seems like every answer to a metaphysical question only raises two more questions *ad infinitum.* And this, as in all aspects of the human predicament, makes you feel limited when you don't know the truth you yearn for. You feel as though you almost have it, just a little more stretching, and then comes more limitation in the human predicament through the search for truth.

However, there is one absolute, final, and ultimate truth available that includes all other relative truths. The catch-22 of it is that to understand the absolute truth, you can't use the mind but have to absorb it with intuitive knowing, which transcends the mind's ability. This kind of intuitive knowing that I call Pearl Vision is available after awakening. Onions just don't ever get it! Another catch-22 is that to place that absolute truth out there for you to even hear it, we have to put it in words, which immediately converts it back to a relative truth. But that's only a problem for onions, not Pearls.

As far as I know, only one sage ever put this absolute truth out there after his awakening. That was Ramana Maharshi, who was the epitome of simplicity. The following might be considered as his scripture, for those who like that idea. He says:

"There is no creation or dissolution.
There is no path or goal.
There is no free will or predestination."

That's it! That is the only absolute truth. Here is what this absolute statement means in relative terms: There is only Consciousness as Source.

Source is either unmanifest at rest, or Source
is manifest in appearance.
When Source is in appearance, It is in the
form of a dream.
When you are experiencing a dream, you
cannot say that what is happening is real,
no matter how realistic it may seem.

As Source goes into appearance, It manifests
Itself in the *creation* of the universe.
As Source goes back to rest, it *dissolves* its
manifest creation.
While in this appearance, it is part of the
human predicament to look for and follow
a *path* that leads to a specific goal, either
God as a spiritual goal, or total abundance
as a material goal.
Locked into the human predicament, man
feels as though he has *free will* to pick his
life's choices.
Yet the awakened ones tell us that all is a
matter of *predestination* and destiny.
So, in this dream of appearance, we can

transcend the relative truth that Source
first creates and then dissolves the
creation.
Having thus transcended this creation,
obviously there is no longer any issue
about free will versus predestination, nor
any need for paths or goals.

What Ramana is saying here, is that if you get confused by
the contradictions that lie in all relative truths because they are
part of duality, and all opposite polarities meet in the middle to
cancel each other out, then not to worry! Just go one step
beyond all relative truths in the final absolute truth that none of
this ever really happened at all, because relative dreams don't
count as absolute reality.

Here is a perspective of Pearl Vision to explain all of the
outrageously conflicting "truths" that one hears during a lifetime of dealing with the human predicament. Everyone has
their own relative truth that they not only speak but also act on.
This truth and action may terribly affront us and we may see
through the speciousness of their truth and regard their actions
as ruthless. An example of this could be a Middle-Eastern
Islamic terrorist whose truths cause chaos and destruction to
some Israelis. Yet I can see there is an inner logic to what that
terrorist says that is known only to him. Not only does he have
inner logic for his statements and actions, but that logic or "relative truth" is coming directly and only from Source, as a very
intense expression of the human predicament that Source
enjoys so much. So, as you encounter daily the many outrageous and conflicting truths proposed, you can smile at the cosmic joke of it all and say a silent "Namaste" to each and every
one with deep respect for the Source behind that "truth."

Once this one absolute truth discussed here became a central theme of my deliverance, my search for all relative truth was
over. All relative truths or knowledge had become so burdensome as to be uncomfortable to deal with anymore. It was sort of

like going on a long car trip. We have luggage with us. We can set that luggage down on the floor for the duration of the trip or put it all on top of our head. Either way we are going to end up at the exact, same destination; one way totally exhausted from carrying all that weight, the other relaxed and carefree because all that junk rode on the floor. That's pretty much how all words, knowledge, and theories affect me now. I enjoy the utter simplicity of this one absolute truth, and all other relative truths are now irrelevant. Ah! Life is good!!

CHAPTER 35

FREEDOM

As I mentioned early on in this story of awakening and deliverance, the importance of freedom is the cornerstone of the rapture. It was the first feedback that something very sudden and dramatic had happened to my normal onion conditioning in the human predicament. Just how important this turned out to be was gradually revealed to me over the course of the deliverance.

In my quest for Eastern mysticism, I had hungrily searched out the meaning of enlightenment and how to get there. I studied all the scriptures and all the saints and sages. Rather than listing all the names and teachings, let me attempt to briefly summarize them for you. Most agreed on the experience of Oneness with Source, no matter what they called it. But getting there and then maintaining your connection, or even improving your position afterward, is where I have great difficulty in agreeing with any similarity of a deliverance experience.

You see, even though these sages agree that we are God in essence, there is the underlying assumption that there is everything out there in the universe as One, as God—and then there is me. That really confuses me. Their counsel is to engage in all these disciplines of austerity as a practice of purification. Then there is a heavy emphasis on evil, bad karma, past and subsequent lives in reincarnation, prayer, humility, and infinite do's and don'ts. In one word, limitation into more contraction due to certain types of morality. This kind of deliverance is the norm for sages after their awakening and can come only from Source. What else can I say? Except that I ask you this: Are we possibly at the dawning of a new age of deliverance that revolves around the end of limitation and the beginning of a new freedom?

When I realized that all there is, is Consciousness, it wasn't like there is only Consciousness and then there's little ole me here aware of It. No! Consciousness—I Am That—bye-bye small separated "me." Hello Oneness! So being one with and as Source, I fell head over heels into that vastness of Source at rest where all is truly well, just as it is. Total absolute freedom to relax and let go of any and all ideas of changing or improving anything in the universe to something better, purer, or higher in consciousness. How could it? It's all perfect as is! I kept asking myself: WHAT ARE THESE GUYS TALKING ABOUT? In spite of what they command, I'm not impelled by any inner urge to go feed the hungry, teach the ignorant, or save the addicted ones. Am I now crazy, am I calloused and insensitive to the sufferings of others? I used to believe this stuff, too. Am I delinquent in my own practice by letting go of every spiritual practice I had ever pursued as totally irrelevant now? But all I can feel now is the total freedom from all doing—from all intentional efforting to court Spirit.

Now I can just surrender to the knowing that Source has every detail under control and in the process of lawful unfolding as Destiny. If Source needs me as a particular instrument, then some homeless guy will come to me asking for a meal. Some inquiring mind will ask me to share Satsang. It's also true that I can't refuse when someone does ask me, if I have what they want, because to me, It is Source at play asking me. On the other hand, I can't ask for anything else either, because this same Source already knows what It needs and gives without asking, without me even thinking of what I need.

I can't go out looking for people to fix. The standard Eastern tradition of service to mankind as a path to God does not fit with my new sense of freedom. If Source wants some service, it will happen, with me, without me, in spite of me, and never because of me. There's no need for volunteers, you will hear your name if you are paged over the loudspeaker. Neither do I need to fix any of the predispositions within my own genetic and DNA personality makeup. If Source wants me any different, old habits and conditioning will just naturally fall away like dead skin. I've already watched this happening the last few years. No more self-imposed, self-help techniques to better my position with Source. I Am Source, exactly as I am! Why would I want it any different?

Do you get a flavor here of the kind of freedom that now sustains me at every moment? The change in experience from extreme limitation to total freedom was so sudden and so complete that, when I tried to explain it to those who knew me best, I met with stares of incredulity. At times I thought myself crazy from too much of the psychotic conditions present in that county jail. But you cannot argue or doubt the nonending, ever-increasing peace and joy of this rapture. That is my best validation, besides the experience itself, that this freedom is real, not delusional, and flows from the awakening of the realization of who I am. If that's being crazy, then we live in a mad world within the rapture.

I challenge you to find this freedom described in any traditional teaching or any conventional wisdom that does not include the need for additional service, Satsang, and meditation. We mentioned earlier that the New Agers are expecting this radical shift in the consciousness of the planet. They are expecting a massive ascension process to free us from the human predicament. Who knows? Maybe they are right about a change, but could it be that Source is now introducing a new element in the lawful unfolding? Could that change be in the freedom from conditioning that says we have to change ourselves and others to something better than what is? Is this the beginning of the end of karma? Is this the signal for Source changing the rules of engagement for limitation in our human predicament?

Instead of the New Age, let's call it the age of freedom. The law of Moses birthed the age of karma with an eye for an eye, a tooth for a tooth! Buddha birthed the age of compassion. Jesus birthed the age of brotherly love. Mohammed's main message was mercy—ours is the age of freedom. Freedom that doesn't prostrate us with grief at the sufferings of others, because there are no others. There's only Source as I Am, dreaming the play of limitation in the human predicament.

But didn't I say that everyone's life and every situation in that life is balanced with a Freedom/Limitation equation? So, if freedom is the all-pervasive experience of the rapture these days, then where is the balance of the limitation? The limitation here is: There is no one home to personally enjoy the freedom. That's why, if you could choose between having 10 million dollars or an awakening, take the money and run! At least there will be somebody home to enjoy it for a while!

I remember so vividly, during the awakening process, the delicious shivers of delight and the giggles running through me when I realized the futility of any attempt to pursue a path of spiritual discipline. Concomitant with this realization was an immediate falling away of my pursuit of seeking distractions to relieve boredom. Before prison, it was more like hedonism, but that's not even an option behind these walls. Those first rushes of freedom crashing over me like a breakwater in the surf—constant and refreshing. The search and effort are over! Whether or not I change one more iota in my spiritual quest, not only is it not up to "me," not only is it not possible using intentional effort or will power, but also it isn't even relevant. There isn't even a "me" to improve!

In that first rush of freedom, I could see the intrinsic value of Saddam Hussein causing enormous chaos in the Middle East, alongside the balance of Mother Theresa caring for the lepers in India. It is all the same to Source. If I could somehow change any disaster in the world or create a better situation through my free will, I would be causing Source enormous stress. It would now have to redesign the entire universe to offset this new factor because it wasn't in the original design. How dare I? What presumption!

With freedom comes the knowing that there is no place in the universe, from cathedral to brothel, that has any more or less consciousness present than any other place. There is no activity any more or less spiritual than any other, because all doing is done by Source. There is no ambience that attracts or repels spirit more, because it is all Spirit. Just to be, doing nothing, is as much the Presence of Source as feeding all the hungry of the world.

Let me make this more real for you by citing some actual experiences. The backdrop is the prison yard. Scene I: I am out the door every morning at 6:00 A.M. so I can get some peace and quiet time for meditation over in the corner of the yard. Halfway through a blissful purring of Presence, a trio of young gang bangers comes over to my exact spot because it is the farthest place away from "the man." They engage in loud hip-hop jive, all talking at once. Deliverance gears start shifting automatically. Now, instead of having a quiet meditation, Source evidently wants to party a little. So we symbolically reach out in Presence to embrace the intruders as part of the meditation process that has now changed from a purring to a street rap. Source is equally present in both situations. But onion conditioning says that a quiet meditation is more conducive to spiritual growth than revelry. Pearl Vision sees only the Presence of Consciousness as equally at play in both scenarios, just under different appearances.

Scene II (still the most vivid in my memory): My taste in music runs more to classical than to pop and I shudder at the sound of heavy metal. After two years locked up in the county jail with nothing but "gangsta rap" playing on boom boxes 24/7, I suffer post-traumatic stress syndrome every time I hear it now. So one day after the wake-up call, I was meditating in a quiet corner and someone came up with loud rap music playing on a radio speaker and sat down right next to me. I then felt the embrace by Source of that cacophony in my inner space, and so I was operating on a dual level. One part, still in the awareness of Presence, and another part, allowing rap to be a part of the

Presence. All of a sudden, the whole scene became an out-of-body experience when I heard the rap music turn into the most beautiful celestial sounds and colors that were not any part of my previous human experience. In total awe, I was trying to figure out what was happening, when I heard a clear, inner voice say: "This is how Source hears rap music!" I got it! That experience did not help me to appreciate rap music any more than before, because it's still coming through as a third-dimensional sound. But it did deepen the understanding of allowing what is—as is into my awareness as being exactly as it should be.

One more example of this freedom: Let's say you wake up one morning and you usually meditate at this time, but this morning, instead of meditating, you feel like you would rather go cross-country skiing. Which is better for your "spiritual quest?" To Source, they are identical and you can relax without guilt if you end up skiing instead of meditating. First of all, this is all hypothetical, because you don't have the freedom of choice to decide anyway. Source is going to move you the way of Its lawful unfolding, whichever way that happens to be. Your freedom comes in knowing that Source is pulling the strings. You are more in touch with reality if you go skiing, knowing that Source is the doer, than if you stayed home and meditated, unaware that this meditation was being done by Source, but thinking you were sacrificing fun so you could earn spiritual points in your quest.

That is why a yearning for God, or spirituality, is exactly the same as a yearning for a million dollars. They both come from the misunderstanding of the separated self as a "me," looking for something outside of "me," whether that be God or material gain.

So my dear brothers and sisters, this may well be the first time in your life that you are getting the real message and flavor of freedom. Some awakened ones have left messages of how they lived their lives after awakening as a guidepost of do's and don'ts for you to emulate. Basically, it is a recommendation of turning away from all sense objects and stressing the impact of karma—good or bad—on life's progress. But the age of karma is now over. It never really existed except as a concept of conditioning you inherited in the human predicament. I'm telling you now that in my freedom experience of Source as One, as the only "doer" involved in existence, it doesn't matter to Source what role we are playing as a projection of Source. It is all the same! We can just relax now and giggle at the huge cosmic joke we see all around us in our newfound age of freedom. If you carry only one message away with you from this journal, it is this:

> You are free to be exactly as you are
> right now.
> Any changes in your makeup will come
> from Source.
> Everything is exactly the way it should be—
> all is well—all is good!

CHAPTER 36

WASTED TIME

The most common complaint I heard in prison from the inmates, was how much frustration (limitation) they felt over the years "wasted" in prison. Time that had been taken from them when they could have been "doing" something more productive. Time was now lost that could never be recouped, their youth robbed from them, replaced with old age and the bitter memories of being locked up.

This same scenario is a replay for all of those trapped by the human predicament in a situation where they might be permanently immobilized by injuries or degenerative diseases. They feel their time and life are wasted because they have lost an important part of their freedom, their mobility in a healthy body. They feel worse off than even the prisoners, for at least there is some light for inmates at the end of the tunnel, if they are not serving life sentences. How about all the millions of entities trapped into a life situation where they feel stuck, like in subpoverty, the ghettos, war zones, famine zones, dead marriages, dead-end jobs? All just "wasting time" in a survival mode. Of course, Source is able to milk an enormous ongoing experience of limitation from all those dealing with the wasted time syndrome. And yet, I mention this topic only because I'm sure that the nature of my deliverance was influenced by waking up in a "wasted time" zone environment—prison.

When I was first arrested, the oppression of dead time weighed very heavily on me. Like everyone else, I felt crushed by it. I went from cruising around the world in my private plane and sailboat to living for two years with 32 people in a room the size of the average kitchen. There was nothing to do, nowhere to go, and just breathing the suffocating heat and body smells made one weak. But I felt the greatest uncomfortable pressure not from the physical discomforts, nor even from trying to survive in a ghettolike war zone, but from the loss of valuable time—forever down the tubes!

Once the wake-up call and deliverance kicked in, all that drastically changed. The "dead time" factor shifted from producing high anxiety and additional stress to a new sense of gratitude for each moment of awareness, aliveness, and a sense of Presence in original innocence regained. And yes, within the very same environment and conditions of oppressive prison life.

Imagine the human predicament being a veil covering over this pure Pearl of Consciousness that we are. Suddenly the veil is removed. We can now see clearly what before was invisible or very obscured. What would we now see?

> We see that consciousness is equally everywhere and totally present in this very moment and situation.

> We see that there is no greater concentration of "higher energy," say in Sedona, Arizona, than in the prison cell block.

> We see that there is not a situation that is more or less conducive to the full import of inner wisdom than any other.

> We see that there is nothing to do, or not do, within the framework of the human predicament.

> We see that just being here, as an alive instrument of Source, is enough.

> We see that understanding and the awareness of who we are, together with feeling the Presence of Source, becomes the core issue of existence.

> We see that "dead time" is a valuable ally to step out of distractions and relax into this understanding.
>
> We see that the rapture of being swept away from all the illusory concerns of the human dramas comes from the eternal spring of Source within the center of all this "wasted time."

When we not only see, but also feel and know this intuitively, then every situation—in or out of prison—in or out of a wheelchair—in or out of a substance abuse center—becomes the same. Instead of running around the world to visit the most beautiful reserves of nature, we can stay in one place, be quiet, and enjoy the Source who projects all this beauty, right here, right now, unconditionally! Sometimes I marvel that I am still in a human body after this awakening. By lifting this veil of conditioning, Source has now basically handicapped Its experience of limitation through the vehicle of my mind/body organism.

If there is anyone reading these words now who has to deal with his/her version of "wasted time," whether it be a minor situation like gridlock in traffic, or as a lifelong quadriplegic with a respirator, know that the Source of all freedom, joy, and beauty lies within your very awareness, which can read and understand these concepts. Time is a given in our experience of the human predicament to embrace what is—as is, and as is means *exactly as it should be!*

If you were born into the human predicament, it means you will have to deal with this issue of feeling stuck and frustrated during periods of more or less "wasted time." This is as it should be! It means that Source is doing well in Its design for us human projections. It does not mean we have to resist and struggle to change the situation, get out of it, or, if nothing else works, just lose ourselves in distraction until it's over. If by some miracle of Grace, you feel you haven't had to deal with this yet, you still have the decrepitude of old age to look forward to. But not to worry! In this area, as in every situation of the human predicament, there is always the balance of freedom built into every limitation.

What happened to me in dealing with the so-called "dead time" of prison is funny. If you saw that movie *Ghost*,[1] you might relate to my description more. After Patrick Swayze gets killed, he wanders around as a disincarnate spirit, aware of all sense objects, but unable to interact with them. This drives him crazy with frustration, because he wants to save his fiance from harm, and is impotent at first. In my deliverance after the death of the ego personality in the wake-up call, I felt like that spirit wandering around the confines of the prison. But I was not trying to change or better anything. I felt like I was on a special mission from Spirit to just report conditions on earth, in this specific prison. Not to judge them, or compare them, or have an opinion about them, or even have a preference about the options. In short, a ghost who was a silent witness in choiceless awareness of life in the Big House. With Grace and deliverance, this new role was so delightful after a lifetime of resisting what is—to what I want it to be. So in this house of horrors, I found joy. I laughed till I cried at the cosmic joke of it all. And in the end, I finally realized that it didn't matter if I ever got out. It's all the same anyway, wherever you are. I Am That!

---

[1] *Ghost*, Paramount Pictures, 1990.

CHAPTER 37

"WHO SAYS WORDS WITH MY MOUTH?" — RUMI[1]

Most self-help books you have ever read, and most work-shops or seminars you have ever attended, have left you with workable principles to deal with the goals in mind. I have already declared my intention to have this book be a story about awak-ening and not a path to achieve it. However, it can leave you with some indicators of where you are in the human predicament.

Remember, all individual mind/body organisms are born into the human predicament. This is as constant as the law of gravity. It is always present because we have an intellect whose function it is to judge, and judgment places us in the human predicament. But within the human predicament are various layers or levels of comfort and discomfort. These levels are deter-mined by whether we are judging and resisting what is—as is, or whether we are embracing what is—as is, as a projection of Source. So we can say that awareness and surrender are the more or less most natural states of someone who has awakened.

But this deliverance from the conditioning of a previous lifetime of judging everything, and resisting what we don't like, does not happen overnight. After the wake-up call, we often find ourselves in a situation where we are enjoying a sense of Presence, the rapture of Source, when suddenly we become aware of someone else speaking words through our brain that sure sound like a summary judgment of what's hap-pening. In fact, those kind of words are often accompanied by pangs of discomfort, because we have slipped out of the choiceless awareness role of the witness. Now, does that mean we are not intimately connected to Source during our little side trip of judging? No. It only means that Source is delving into the human predicament again through our mind/body organism, for whatever reason. But this time it's different! We stay connected because we know what is happening and the pang of sudden discomfort is only an indicator of Source's movement through us. It gives us an opportunity to take a deep breath of awareness and fall back again into the vastness of Source. It's like a gentle nudge from Source to reaffirm that Source is the only energy present, and the only doer in that offensive person in front of us. Instead of taking a step backward in consciousness with our little judgment, we have actually moved forward in awareness of Source.

A person still sleeping in the ignorance of preconditioning has no idea why he/she suddenly feels uncomfortable with passing thoughts, namely, the words transmitted by Source to the receiver of his/her brain. This Source is like the light energy that is coming off the sun into his/her brain. If it is received directly, it comes in as pure white, healing light. If it is received through the prism of the mind, it refracts into a distortion of multiple shapes and unfamiliar colors. But the point is, this is the same light either way. And awareness of image with the distortion of resistance, or the direct acceptance of it as Source, is the same awareness of Source—either way!

So when Source starts speaking through your brain and it causes judgment and discomfort, know that all is well and be grateful for the awareness of this as it happens. It's part of the deliverance and definitely diminishes with the passage of time. It's the awareness of what's up that is the litmus test of Source, not what's happening through you.

The story you are reading here is directed to you as an assurance that those of you who are now ready to jump out of this airplane of your preconditioning into the open but scary space of nondoing at what seems like 30,000 feet, with no parachute or safety net, will land intact. What I am here to tell you from actual experience is that if you relax into nondoing as a life attitude, you will not crash and burn. There is definitely a safety net of Source sustaining the lawful unfolding of your destiny. You ask me, "But how do I run a business, a home, or a life with nondoing as an attitude of surrender? How do things get done?" Well, I can assure you that if you pay attention to what is occurring and are resting in the knowing that you are absolutely not the doer, or a free-choice agent, you will observe the following: Everything that is supposed to happen will happen! Things just get done, with or without you, in spite of you, rather than because of you. You find yourself getting up, moving, phoning, saying words, and the whole time knowing that it is Source operating through you. In the beginning, it's fine to operate "as if" you are the doer, so long as you know in your heart that it's just not so. After time and deliverance, you remain on auto pilot all the time. You definitely know who is driving this vehicle, and acting "as if" you are the doer becomes irrelevant.

This attitude of nondoing promotes an attitude of detachment about the results of what you are attempting to do. If you are not the doer, and you are not attached to the outcome of the project, only one role is left—a witness in choiceless awareness.

I share this with you because I'm sure from my own journey that the constant peace and freedom I experience in the rapture is flowing out of this life-spring of nondoing, nonintentional efforting. And when you find yourself hanging out in this swept-away sensation of freedom, you too can muse with Rumi with a twinkle in your eye: "Who is saying these words with my mouth?"

[1] Star, J. and S. Shiva (Eds.), *Garden beyond Paradise: The Mystical Poetry of Rumi.* New York: Bantam Books (1992).

CHAPTER 38

ARE WE HAVING FUN YET?

Now that you have finished this tale of madness and freedom, perhaps you are asking yourself: "What does it all mean?" Rather than trying to put a meaning to it, why not ask yourself if you now feel any different about life. You will know that our journey together has been engaged at the intuitive level if your overall feeling is one of tremendous relief. No conclusions to follow, just outrageous freedom tugging at your heart. Does it feel like the weight of the world has been lifted off your chest? That's how much all your layers of conditioning have weighed on you. So for the last time here, let's run by the reasons that you feel so much relief:

> You no longer need to be the doer.
>   It's already handled.
> Forget all intentional efforts.
> You can't screw up.
> You can't lose out.
> You are not responsible for saving the world.
> You can't make a wrong choice.
> You will accomplish your destiny.
> You are enlightened at your core essence.
> It really doesn't matter whether you are
>   awakened or not.
> You can't be a victim.
> You have no enemies out there. Only Source!
> You can forget about bad "karma." It's over
>   and never existed!

No mystery of what you will be in your next
life. There is no you!
You don't have to worry about the purpose
of life. With infinite wisdom, Source has
laid out the design of your life.
The more you can just be in nonintentional
efforting, the better the inner tube floats
down the white water of life. Inner tubes
do not require oars or a rudder!
Witnessing life in choiceless awareness is the
most fun—relaxed, peaceful, satisfying
and exciting in every way possible in this
human predicament journey.
Since Source is the only doer, that lets you
off the hook as God's little helper.
By the end of the journey, no matter what
you did or didn't do, achieved or did not
achieve, the ultimate outcome is still all
the same—at rest again in Source.
No matter how difficult you may perceive
your life situation, it is always in perfect
balance of freedom to limitation. It is no
better or worse off than anyone else's, just
different, that's all!
What we have all taken so seriously all our
lives is really part of a very funny joke.
You are perfect exactly as you are right now.
In fact, everything is exactly the way it
should be, and nothing needs to be fixed
or changed.

Now when you hear the inner chatter of negativity about
a person or situation, you can relax back into awareness and
know that what is really going on is only Source in appearance.

CHAPTER 39

RIOTS AND REFLECTIONS

We just came out of an extended lockdown, not only at this prison at Terminal Island, but in all the federal prisons that were locked down because of nationwide rioting. I witnessed inmates and guards engaged in mortal combat, the inevitable outcome of severe overcrowding and harsh drug penalties that are 100 times more severe for blacks than whites (blacks now number 61 percent of all prison populations). I watched whole housing units burned and destroyed with unbelievable rage and fury. As I lay in that hard metal bunk for weeks awaiting some semblance of prison normalcy, Satsang from Source was virtually uninterrupted, in spite of the horrific noise level accompanying the constant yelling and screaming 24/7. Now that the cells are open again, I can share these "riot reflections" with you.

Playing with Source is so unpredictable! Just when you think: "Okay, that feels like enough for now," along comes something new to push against you for new insights. That's the beauty of the human predicament—there will always be change to guarantee both diversity and evolution. Let's discuss both of these terms.

Diversity

You may have noticed that throughout this story I have been emphasizing Source's insatiable quest for limitation. But really, that is only half of the story. The other half, and equally as important to observe, is Source's quest for diversity through the entire appearance of creation in general and through the human predicament in particular. In our role of embracing all of created reality as is, it's helpful to understand this role of diversity in the world of Source's appearance.

Both science and our own awareness tell us that everything in this world is a one of a kind, unique creation. This is especially apparent now through the study of DNA differences within the same species. Source not only doesn't project sameness in Its creations of appearances, but It also doesn't engender boring sameness within the various experiences of the human predicament. As I witness Source projected out into appearance, I am constantly amazed at the diversity of the One within the actions, both bizarre and beautiful, of the many. I can see a situation out of the normal and then the voice of deliverance whispers to me: "Ah, here is Source, playing Its game of infinite diversity again." But before the wake-up call, that same situation may have triggered something like "What is that weirdo's problem?" Prison is a true microcosm of the big world out there. I get to watch Source as every character, race, and personality imaginable. What a boring world if everyone thought and acted like everyone else! I can imagine a scenario of melting back into Beingness at death where there is a kind of brief Academy Awards presentation for having lived whatever role you pretended to be in as an outstanding life performance—the violent gang bangers and prison guards, blacks and whites, all throwing flowers at each other as they fade together into the Oneness of Source again. Which one did a better job in its respective role of a freedom/limitation balancing act in search of diversity? Well, actually, each was an act of perfection and sure had everyone else fooled! So when onion vision wants you to have reality conform to your limited view of the human predicament, that is a very good time to peel that layer away into the mysterious *diversity* of what is–as is.

Evolution

The other word to explore here is *evolution*. Everyone assumes we are evolving as a planet into higher consciousness.

I agree! But not because that means higher consciousness is a better evolution than lower consciousness. It just so happens that spiraling down in evolution doesn't work. Compare it to the law of gravity. Gravity could conceivably work in either direction. In reverse, objects could fly off the face of the earth toward outer space if that was the way Source projected it. But that would not be very practical, because everything would constantly be flying up and away instead of falling down and staying on the planet. So, down isn't better than up, it just works better in the specific case of gravity. So it is with evolution. Because Source loves diversity, It guarantees perpetual diversity in the human predicament by constant change. So we have to deal with constant change in our patterns of moving through life. If we evolve downward, we soon end up at the animal level or worse, and that is the end of the human predicament. But if we evolve higher into consciousness, then there is no limit and evolution goes on indefinitely. That works better!

So when onion vision tells you that this situation is a necessary lesson in order to learn about life and the evolution into higher consciousness, don't believe it. Source doesn't need to learn lessons about life. Source just loves diversity—therefore, constant change—therefore, an evolution that takes place in the only direction possible—higher. Nothing mysterious or esoteric about this. Peel it away and know that Source is just playing and amusing Itself through the diversity that comes with evolution.

Lies and Exaggeration

One of the interesting side effects of awakening and deliverance that takes place is the process of rewinding the entire video of your life up to this point and playing it again in slow motion to relive those same events from the perspective of Pearl Vision. This happens spontaneously in quiet alone time and is actually quite enjoyable. You get to see how distorted your vision of life was as an onion, and how delicious it feels as the Pearl that you really are—now totally free in the midst of the human predicament. But along with this freedom, you also experience the embarrassment of seeing all those acts of limitation and contraction that occurred here and there along the way.

Through this process, it became clear to me that any time in my life I had resorted to a lie or exaggerated the situation, it was because I was in resistance to what is–as is and wanted to present a better situation that was more along the lines of what I wanted or needed. Maybe I could make it better if only I presented myself in a more favorable light. Maybe they would think better of me with a lie than the way it truly was. Once the awakened view of Pearl Vision takes over, who cares anymore what anyone else thinks! This is what is! It's all Source in appearance anyway, so a detachment develops around what is and to anyone's reaction to my description of any unpleasant facts. Describing a scene factually is now my way of embracing that reality more fully. The highest priority is not fixing it or making it more appealing, but embracing what is–as is—as Source in appearance. The same holds true if you have something that I don't have but want. Attempting to take it from you, without your offering it, is again resistance to what is. So it all boils down to Pearl Vision again. Seeing yourself and all others as One and the same Source. Knowing that you can't possibly figure it all out with your teeny limited mind, and then surrendering to all of it as is—as a projection of Source. What a constant rush!

Fountain of Wisdom

In exploring and presenting this so-called wisdom that I call Pearl Vision, what have I glimpsed that is truly worthy of wisdom itself? Only this: However liberating and exciting this shedding of onion vision has been in the emergence of awakening and deliverance, it is still just one unique experience of Source in Its quest for diversity. I know that whatever has been presented so far comes directly from the fount of all wisdom—Source. Yes, other people's truths may definitely contradict ours and each others. Yes, some of them may feel very distasteful to our sensibilities. But because of their Source, they all are relatively true, which means I now revere whatever I hear, from whatever so-called fanatical voice, as sacred a truth as my own inner voice. It doesn't mean I believe it or try to incorporate what others say into my life. I just respect it as their sacred truth—as important to Source in Its quest for diversity, as the truth It has revealed through me. No one is ever wrong or false in his/her teachings! It may not be true for anyone else in the universe, but it is certainly true for them. So I embrace whatever I hear now as what is, sacred to them, without any judgment or opinion from me.

This enables me to draw two more conclusions about the human predicament. The only real teacher you can have is your own unique voice of wisdom—to which everyone has access within themselves. Other teachers can only present an alternative to what your conditioning has already taught you. Whether it is true or not for you depends on your bodily response. If you shudder and feel repulsed, then obviously, it's not your truth. But if you feel excited and attracted, then maybe you can explore it more deeply, and allow your own fount of wisdom to develop it. The bottom line is, the buck stops right here! You, and you alone, are the source of all the wisdom that is ever needed in your sojourn through the human predicament. Whatever you glean out of life is precisely the truth that Source wanted to experience in your unique mind/body organism. You can't be wrong in whatever truth you embrace, no matter how disastrous it may appear. It is all coming from Source. Everyone is absolutely sacred in the truth of their own unique brand of wisdom.

The second conclusion from our fount of wisdom: Since everyone's truth is sacred, so are the actions inspired by this truth. If your truth as a gang-banger growing up in the ghetto is to take what you want, and the end justifies the means, well, that is a perfect expression of Source in Its role of living Its unique truth as a perfect gang-banger. This is as sacred a role as the venerable monks whose only truth in life is the Catholic church, celibacy, and selfless service to others. Their roles and actions evolve from whatever relative truth that Source is feeding and feeling in each of them respectively. No better, no worse, no more true, no less true. All Source—the One in the diversity of the many. All perfect as is! To try to fix anyone's truth or actions would be to ruin them. Each has the very same fount of wisdom, only in a different expression.

As an integrating part of my deliverance, this point was brought home to me by Source in the appearance of Hector. Hector is this little old bald-headed Latino who jogs around here at the incredible speed of two miles per hour, and he can sustain it for hours every day. He is a born-again Christian Fundamentalist who is carried away with enthusiasm for proselytizing to anyone who is willing to hear about hell, final judgment and eternal damnation. His daily routine out in the rec yard in the mornings is to jog around looking for prospective converts, hand them a printed message for the day, and then give them a pep talk. I used to submit to jogging visits every day from Hector, not because I needed a Biblical briefing, but because it made Hector feel so good to have someone to preach to. All I had to do was accept the brochure and nod in agreement, and Hector was swept away in the delight of preaching the Lord's word. So, one day I am in my usual remote corner of the yard meditating, and I look up to see Hector jogging in place right there in front of me, giving his usual spiel about the danger of Satan. But lo and behold, all I could see was Hector bathed in the most incredible golden light, with a face more beautiful than any angel's. I couldn't say a word, but tears started streaming down my face in recognition of Source in appearance. I'm sure Hector thought I was touched by his message of fear, but I knew instantly that his truth was as sacred as mine. Quite opposite in content—but sacred and from the same Source. After that incident, I could never look at Hector again without a silent "Namaste" and a knowing smile of recognition.

Follow Your Bliss

One of the central themes I encountered throughout my searching in New Age philosophy was the admonition to "follow your bliss" as a means to enlightenment. This is a great idea in theory but when it came to reasons why I pursued my various pet projects, the motivation always seemed to boil down to need, greed, lust, and dependency. If any bliss was ever involved, it was too momentary to be of any significance.

In the deliverance that followed the wake-up call, I began to understand this "follow your bliss" on two different levels. With the understanding that, since Consciousness is all there is, then whatever I'm involved in doesn't bring me eternal rewards, whether it's good service to others, or bad karma if I am self-gratifying in my pursuit of conventional goals. Real bliss, as love, abundance, and true power (mastery over self), is the natural outcome of knowing who I am, and not goals to be pursued. Fear can never be considered as motive for any objective, either. So in the first wave of understanding, it was clear to me that since it really doesn't matter in terms of personal or cosmic repercussions what I do to get by in life, I might as well "follow my bliss" and only be involved in what is most enjoyable to my unique, inherited predispositions, in other words, that which makes me feel most alive in a positive way. A simple example: Maybe it "seems" like there is a fork in the road where taking one path means making a lot of money selling "stuff," but the other path appears to be more delightful because there you get to do something that doesn't pay as much but is more enjoyable. "Following my bliss" would indicate that I go where work is play. But that is too simple, because Source decides which fork to go down by causing us to be more attracted to one road than the other.

So let's talk about the second level of understanding the meaning of "following your bliss." With more deliverance and a deeper understanding of Consciousness in motion, a more subtle understanding has emerged. It seems now that it doesn't have anything to do with either doing or not doing. When

167

Grace has permeated your whole being and you view this world of appearance through the eyes of Source, an attitude of "nondoing,"of simply witnessing events without opinions, judgments or preferences, takes over. Then, as events transpire, regardless of how they fit your comfort or discomfort mode, the attitude of embracing everything that is – as is becomes the only approach to following your bliss. Source is bliss! Remember the ancients who named Source "Satchitananda?" Well, ananda is the total bliss aspect. Whatever is happening is exactly what Source wants to happen, precisely in the fashion, time, and manner in which it is happening. So as the ego personality that causes the separation and limits the experience is transcended, the *natural result* is Source as Michael embracing Source as destiny, or Source in appearance. Source embracing Source has to equal pure bliss! To be very specific, if you forget about "doing" and your awareness is only focused on embracing whatever is happening as Source, then even if it is physically or emotionally uncomfortable, there is a pervading, underlying bliss in your inner and outer being that overrides the human predicament's confusions and conflicts. In other words, this way of following your bliss is freedom within the human predicament. And that feels like the single most important statement that has affected my life and how I regained my original innocence in this whole crazy, incredible story of awakening.

A high security federal prison is not a very fun place to hang out. Here, a successful life program involves just staying alive and out of the hole and the hospital. But since Source uses whatever is at hand, it has been a unique place to follow the deliverance into the rapture. In case I haven't mentioned it yet, the deliverance eventually produces a state of constant awareness, moment to moment, awake or in dream sleep, that Source is all there is. No more spacing out or getting lost in thoughts or fantasies. I can remember countless zazen sessions in a Zen monastery when my mind and thoughts were so crazy and nonstop that I despaired of ever watching them with any semblance of peace and order. Both conventional and onion vision will tell you that "shit happens" in our third dimension. Well, here is a flash for you that "shift happens" in the fourth through Grace. It is a "happening"—a spontaneous shift—and you are suddenly in a peaceful place on the inside looking out, instead of always feeling like you are on the outside looking in. When there is a constant, nonstop awareness of yourself and all else as Source, then embracing what is—as is becomes an attitude of integration and healing. This is definitely following your bliss.

Let's say an event, probably unpleasant as most are in prison, suddenly occurs. First, there is the awareness of it and the feeling it produces. That is followed by a knowing of who I really am, seeing this event as only Source in motion, followed by a distinct buzz of an embracing "Yes! Namaste!"—and then the actual, real bliss that overrides any potential unpleasantness around the situation. I am talking about an overall, neverending peace with as many buzzes of joy as there are events. Can you just imagine? If that is my reality now in a cold-blooded prison of hostility and violence, what is your potential bliss and freedom in a more loving environment once you learn the power of nondoing and embracing what is—as is?

And what activity produces the most bliss for me these days? It seems like just sharing Satsang with others who are also moving into this same space of awakening and freedom. But describing an activity would be following my bliss according to the first level of understanding. The only definition here worth passing on to you is the one in which I am fully conscious and aware that each and every event that takes place within the framework of my attention is really Source in motion. It is, therefore, just perfect and exactly the way it should be. This awareness and understanding of the situation must somehow trigger some sort of chemical reaction or endorphin release in my bliss center so that I am immediately flooded with with both bliss and an ongoing gratitude. And here is the shocker to both conventional and onion wisdom: Uncomfortable or unpleasant events can trigger bliss the same as their counterparts. You almost have to be in prison or a state psycho ward to fully test this outrageous statement as to accuracy and endurance. But then again, I used to feel that just living in the human predicament in the free world was almost the equivalent. Who would have ever thought that the mystery about "following your bliss" is actually just the simplicity of embracing, moment to moment, here and now, what is—as is. It has nothing to do with your activities but everything to do with your awareness of who you are and the surrender to that reality of all being well as is, and exactly as it should be!

CHAPTER 40

MY
"PERFECT"
LIFE

It is Christmas day and traditionally Christmas is rather depressing here in prison. For one thing, we are separated from all loved ones. For another, the media are constantly present, inviting all to celebrate, whereas the most an inmate can do is look at how many years are still left in this oppressive atmosphere. I'm sure you get the picture. But not so for me today. I went out to the yard as soon as the doors opened at 6:00 A.M. for my usual fitness workout. But instead of jumping on the fitness stepper to kick-start my endorphin level, there was a pull on me to just sit on the ground and quietly meditate for a while. I did this and what then followed was the most wonderful and incredible Christmas gift I could have ever imagined.

It was clear to me that today is a special occasion in this process of deliverance. Today my ultimate destiny was clearly apparent in a flash of insight and recognition, perceived and felt as a gift from Spirit. This insight had been building for months and I had just written more about the topic of regarding everyone else's truth, statements, attitudes, and actions as sacred and flowing out of Source in motion. I had explained how I embraced all situations as they were occurring, and seeing them as Source in motion, which resulted in a buzz of bliss, no matter how negative the scenario appeared. This was a warm-up exercise in the months preceding today's last piece of the puzzle apparently fitting into this so-called mystery of life.

Remember when we played the imaginary game of co-creator and fixed all of the perceived ills of the planet? Well, let's do it again, only this time let's bring into my life every imaginable benefit possible: freedom from incarceration, billions of dollars, fame and power, and so on, *ad infinitum*. But because everything mentioned here is something outside of my own essence, that means that nothing in itself could bring about this total and lasting fulfillment, joy, freedom, and peace I am experiencing.

This is where the gift of today's revelation comes in. What Source has given me here is the Grace of a permanent attitude to see with awareness and embrace with consciousness every single event in life as my own essence in reflection and in motion. When it is an impersonal event, I feel a giant "Yes—So Be It!" It's almost like a sneeze in my inner being. When it is a personal situation involving another, I feel an all-embracing "Namaste!" That's it! That's all there is to it! Nothing else to do in life to make it change for the better. Nothing else to reach out or hope for. My destiny, as I see it today, is just to be and embrace everything else as Source. I have already been experiencing that when Source embraces Source as is, there is only bliss. This results in a *perfect life!* Since I am scheduled to leave this prison life very soon, the thought may have been floating around in my head as to where to go and what to do next. So this was a gift today. An answer—a perfect life, here or anywhere, now and always, regardless of what mode of activity I may find myself in. All I have to do for a perfect life is *nothing!* Just be—alive—aware—conscious of every movement as Source—as is—as perfect—and enjoy the bliss and deeply fulfilling freedom I already have. As simple as breathing.

Now, I realize this insight is my own unique destiny and not a world movement. But I want to share it with you also. Maybe there is something here that can spill over into your unique life destiny. You know that Source uses whatever is at hand, and here we are, involved in sharing a story together. Who knows?

The reason this insight is so full of impact is that I have already been experiencing this kind of breakthrough for over two years. This is sort of like the final vision of what life, my life at least, is really all about. The signposts have all been pointing this way since the beginning of the awakening, and now, here I am. The only view I have from here is so beautiful and exciting that it overwhelms me with gratitude. Remember all those masters who said, "What suffering? Just come over where I am and see if you can still experience any suffering out there." Well, it's true! Embracing what is (even if it appears as suffering on the surface) as Source—consciously—without judgment, opinion, or preference—eliminates the polarities, and all that's left is Source embracing Source.

What I am most aware of at this moment is the unbelievable feeling of personal freedom and power I have and am, even though, ironically at this very moment I sit here at the foot of the gun tower, surrounded by three rows of razor wire fences. There was a time when half in jest I predicted over four years ago that I would probably have to stay in prison until I could find it as appealing and beautiful as my mountaintop garden in Costa Rica. Well, that has come to pass now, but it is way beyond the beauty of any place on this planet. I feel such a complete circle of closure today on prison life as I've known it, and some kind of beginning adventure that has nothing to do with either a location or an activity. I actually have nothing here, and yet I am overflowing with a sense of abundance. This is surely the last piece in the puzzle of living a life fulfilled and yet free of all extraneous conditions.

As I examine more carefully this "perfect life," one of its main characteristics is that it lies within the realm of being totally ordinary and simple. Our conditioning through onion vision has emphasized that it is important to be *special*. Much that we strive for is measured and compared with certain norms and the accomplishments of others. We want the best, the most, the greatest, the first in every positive category of life, and we think we know where we are in life only by our comparisons to others. The clarity of Pearl Vision shows that all our efforts to be special only strengthen the ego personality and its delusion of separation from Source. So how difficult would it be to be perfectly ordinary in every respect? Instead of trying to make it all better or reach a goal, how about just relaxing into the comfort of knowing real joy and peace lie in just *being*—not doing—aware that everything is exactly the way it should be! Any attempt to do otherwise is only entering the realm of conflict, disappointment, and eventual loss. The gift here is that being ordinary is infinitely more joyous than being special.

Why do you think the masters, the awakened ones, would often shy away from any demonstration of specialness bestowed on them by their followers? Why did some prefer to hide away in obscurity and just enjoy their great secret of being ordinary? Onion vision would dictate that being special has to be more preferable than the commonness of just being ordinary. But that's why they were spiritual masters. They knew better!

Coming from a background of striving with the greatest intensity possible, I reached out my whole life to excel in every action I ever engaged in. I can tell you from personal experience, the gift of embracing the ordinary is the sweetest, most extraordinary grace possible and is now a key to living my new "perfect life."

We know how special miracles are, but part of the cosmic joke that tickles me is the emphasis we see, hear, and read all over this New Age about the importance of miracles. "Expect a miracle!" says onion vision. "No!" replies Pearl Vision. Again wanting, expecting, or imploring for a miracle takes us out of the realm of being ordinary in our journey through this human predicament. I'm not saying not to celebrate miracles in your life when they occur, just that you don't need them anymore to be special or blessed. Just celebrating life as it occurs—and whatever it brings—is the role of one who has awakened to the secret of a "perfect life."

Completely independent of all circumstances in the human predicament, we, as Source in motion, in appearance, in diversity, have the ability to embrace our creation exactly as it is. It is this embracing in a nondoing, but aware attitude that brings out the bliss that is beyond all understanding, and not the makeover of events to our preference.

At one point in this book I described how every event is the same, even if the opposite situation had occurred because of the freedom/limitation equation that balances all life. But there is a deeper understanding of how it is all the same. Every event can be embraced as Source in motion, as is, and celebrated accordingly. Obviously, as an onion, it is easier to rejoice in the pleasantries of life rather than the misfortunes. But as a Pearl, there comes the enjoyment of viewing everything as Source, and when Source as this particular mind/body organism embraces Source as a particular event, we have the bliss of Source at rest, rather than Source in appearance. So for a life to be perfect, everything that happens in this so-called "perfect life" has to be a source of joy, freedom, and fulfillment. The only way that can happen within the confines of this human predicament is to see beyond the obviousness of the illusion of pain and suffering into the reality of Source behind it, and then embrace everything as is, as Source.

I believe this is the peak experience that Source has in the world of appearance. Often when people have a peak experience, they try to hang onto it, and in so doing, lose it. All attempts to recapture it are futile. But I am describing a peak experience that is constant and imperturbable, and therefore cannot be lost. An attitude of nondoing and embracing what is—as is, is the peak experience that Source employs as a constant, once the freedom of awakening has occurred.

CHAPTER 41

SHIFT
HAPPENS

Someone close to my heart asked me recently for my comments on a New Age novel floating around in which a man attains his awakening in a federal prison cell, and at the end of the story, the whole planet shifts from the third dimension into the fourth. Those who hadn't done their homework were obviously left behind in the third dimension to work out their "bad karma." The "good karma," or enlightened ones, were then operating in a parallel universe in the fourth dimension where everything was just "perfect" for these new little angels. This novel definitely fits the profile for the New Age concept of a fourth-dimensional existence.

At risk of perhaps repeating a lot of what I have already described in my story, I would like to share with you an actual, factual, detailed description of my experience of living daily in the fourth dimension. This transition from the third to the fourth is so dramatic and impactful that there are no fuzzy lines of demarcation where you leave one and live in the other. It's all right there, in your face, in your gut, in your heart—but not in your mind, because that is left behind in the third dimension.

Let me start by defining the very concept of this term—the *fourth dimension.* We start with a pencil-point dot on a piece of paper and call that one-dimensional. Then we look at a photograph, where we see length and width, and we call that two-dimensional. As soon as we add depth, we have the third dimension. So the fourth dimension has to be a reality that transcends everything we see and know in the third. Ghosts and angels used to come to mind, but that was before my entry into this marvelous realm. One of the conditions for entering and dwelling permanently in the fourth is that you have to leave everything you think you know about the third dimension behind you, much as a child leaves behind the things of a child as it emerges into adulthood. They are not only incompatible but once over the line, you suddenly realize that the whole third-dimensional world you were living in was a total illusion anyway.

Is this beginning to sound familiar yet? Well, in my own understanding of the fourth, it is synonymous with the word *enlightenment,* which I never use, because everyone is enlightened by the very fact of his/her birth as a projection of Source. So in keeping with this story, so far the closest word would be *awakening,* or the *wake-up* call. However, this is also a very loaded concept when you use it indiscriminantly, and people will tend to regard you as either an egomaniac or a candidate for the looney bin if you casually mention you are living in an awakened state of being. Few people really know what this fourth dimension is all about yet, so you are less likely to be crucified if your lottery ticket comes up and you just say you shifted into the fourth. And I am seeing more and more tickets cashing out at Satsang right here in prison than I had ever imagined possible. I am hearing more and more intense longing for the bliss and freedom that is present in the fourth.

There is nothing you have learned or seen in the third that can possibly prepare you to understand what living in the fourth dimension is all about. There are practically no carryovers. If you arrived on a planet made of cheese and little green men, you would have more in common than shifting from the third to the fourth. And the reason for this is very simple. Everything in the third dimension is based on *separation.* Mankind as separate from God and separate from each other and all living creatures. All of the world's religions, philosophies, theologies, psychologies, and histories are based on the same foundation—*separation.* As soon as you realize that the foundation of the fourth is the *Oneness* of Source—Source is all there is—everything you experience is Source in appearance, Source in diversity, Source in limitation, Source in the unfolding of a Divine Leela as your only destiny—then you have truly crossed over and shifted dimensions.

Your passport to this new dimension is your total surrender of any possibility of the old third-dimensional notion of having free will or any control over your individual destiny. This is the invisible barrier that prevents seekers of the fourth from actually entering therein as finders. These latter want to hold on to some tiny notion that they still have a say about their little separate identities and events in their lives.

The currency of the fourth is your embracing everything you experience here as pure Source in appearance, which means it doesn't need changing or rearranging in any fashion whatsoever! It is all perfect as it is—no matter how it looks on the surface. How much abundance do you require? Well, the more you can embrace and accept what is–as is, the more currency you have and the more freedom you acquire.

When you first cross over from the third, you are wearing the clothing of a "doer." You see, everything in the third seems to be accomplished by some form of doing through intentional effort. You set goals, you try hard, you accomplish and achieve in measurable ways in order to survive in the third. Those clothes are a joke in the fourth. Here you don the attire of "understanding is all." The only requirement is that you understand that all is a play or appearance of Source, which doesn't require your intentional efforts for anything in the fourth. Source may use your individual mind/body organism to accomplish some part of the lawful unfolding of manifest destiny, but certainly there is no separate ego personality or mind here to help or hinder this process.

So we have our foundation, our passport, our currency, and our new clothes. Where does the fun part begin? Well, someone still living in the third and writing a novel about the fourth is going to give a glorified version of the third as his/her concept of what the fourth must be like. In this particular novel, there would be no "negative" predisposition traits left in personalities once they shifted. That couldn't be further from the truth. Remember, there is no carryover from one dimension to the other. The entrance point to the fourth is when the ego personality, or separate mind, dissolves back into the illusion that it always was. This, in turn, dissolves the creation of fear—the principle antagonist of our fun in life. But it replaces the fear component of the third with the total freedom of the fourth. You have no idea how gloriously fun-filled this total and absolute freedom can feel until you are free from all fear.

Remember, I said back there that there are only two emotions in life from which all the others spring? There's love and there's fear. Love by my definition is embracing what is–as is, as Source. Fear doesn't understand that Source is all there is and therefore is afraid of what it doesn't understand or can't control. So I am talking here about a new emotion that's really fun, and that you have never, ever truly experienced in the third dimension. Freedom!

Freedom from all fear. Freedom to love or embrace everything you connect with in life. Freedom as a delicious safety net surrounding you at all times, no matter what you encounter along the way. Freedom to just be—do nothing—and know that everything is not only taken care of and all is well—but that it is all perfect, even as it is. This is unimaginable and unworkable in the third. What do you mean "do nothing?" How does one live life with an attitude of nondoing? Well, you can't in the third, I'm sorry to say! You have to shift over to the fourth and once there, it is all done magically for you, with no intentional efforts ever needed by you again. Now that's freedom!

And nondoing is really fun, too! You get to be like a starstruck witness in choiceless awareness as your new life unfolds before your very eyes in a truly magical, blissful, peaceful way that can never be understood by those who still hang out in the third dimension. If you are feeling over-whelmed by the urgency of events and responsibilities all around you, know that you are in the illusion created by the third. So when I speak of freedom from the need to do, you can only find it in the fourth, in the bosom of Source, where all is safe and taken care of for you.

We don't need to have a New Age version of the whole planet shifting over into the fourth dimension. All we are going to see are individuals melting away from the illusion of their ego personalities and one by one, entering the fourth. It is more fun like this, anyway. You still get to witness the happenings of the third from a view and understanding of the fourth. It seems to me that if the whole planet suddenly shifted over at once, it would most likely be too boring with all that goody-two-shoes stuff and lack of all conflict all the time. But who am I to say! I'm just one witness who has a predisposition for adventure. This way it's like a nonstop, wonderful movie cartoon you are not only watching, but also participating in and thoroughly enjoying the way it all unfolds without your prior knowledge or control.

When I said there is nothing to prepare you in the third or any carryover to the fourth, I can possibly make a couple of small exceptions that will only make that rule more solid. I have to admit that on a few special ecstasy and/or magic mushroom trips, I had profound insight into the state of being where you felt free from fear, safe, and peaceful. But it ended as soon as the chemical stimulation ran out. Then I would spend all my other drug trips trying to regain that once-in-a-lifetime experience of oneness with all creatures. Good news, fellow travelers! This high is the constant, nonstop and permanent experience of the fourth dimension. I couldn't even imagine ever taking another drug or alcohol trip again, because it would only dull this natural high that permeates every molecule of the fourth.

There were also some pretty intense dreams I had in the third that were portents of the unknown bliss to come. That dream-state joy that seared my heart would awaken me as surely as the terror of a nightmare, because it was so unnatural. I would think, "Surely, there is a state of awareness somewhere in which this kind of bliss is available!" Well again, I have good news. That kind of bliss is natural to the fourth, independent of any triggering events. As you embrace what is—as is, in the fourth, you are filled with the joy of Source as It admires Its Own projection of creation. It doesn't even take a special event to do this. All events do it when you are free from judging, comparing, or having opinions and preferences among and about the events that Source sends your way. Here are some day-to-day details of living in the fourth dimension.

Hum and Glimmer

For me there were sensory differences between the third and the fourth. For one thing, I could feel more than hear a kind of pleasant vibration that feels like a low-level hum. But besides feeling nice, it also served as an alarm system. In the early days of the deliverance, when I would slip out of the here and now by thinking of some future or past event, or whenever any aspect of the ego personality would put in its two-cents worth by focusing on the *me* instead of the *I of Self*, my nice hum would stop! Instantly! Like an alarm system trip wire, it made me realize that suddenly something was off balance. Ahhh, of course! And then the hum would begin again. This awareness apparently uses a hum as part of its properties, at least in this individual mind/body organism.

Another of the properties that is quite disconcerting at first is that visually, your peripheral or nondirect vision includes a golden glimmer to it. But if you try to focus on it, it's gone. This glimmer is the presence of Source in all of Its appearances. For example, I can hear two guys screaming at each other over to the side and actually see them glimmer. If I look more directly at them to check out this shining glimmer, it will disappear unless I adopt a soft gaze kind of vision. There's no doubt for me that this glimmer is the way the fourth keeps me in direct contact with Source in everything I see.

There is one more physical sensation that connects me to

Source in the fourth that I can mention here. Many times a day there are sweet exchanges between Source as my inner fount of wisdom and myself taking place. I may be witnessing some bizarre or ruthless behavior, and Source comes through as the gentlest of Satsang to assure me that not all that's happening out there in the third is what it seems on the surface. Consequently, there is this response back from my inner knowing that all is well here, and I can embrace the situation as it is, even though I may not know the inner logic or reason for it. In this mutual dance and embrace we do, there comes a flutter of warmth and excitement in the pit of my stomach. The only feeling comparable to this in a generic sense, and this may sound silly, is perhaps the intensity of puppy love you felt once as a teenybopper. It sort of knocks you over with a giddiness. You know you are onto something big here, like a special secret you are sharing, and you just tingle all over. Sometimes this sensation is so strong that for a few moments I feel almost dysfunctional. But maybe these bouts of intensity help to sustain the deep, abiding sense of peace that doesn't ever let up.

Dream State

Even though you are aware of flipping back and forth between the third and fourth dimensions in the early part of deliverance, time heals all the seeming separation, and eventually you are only aware of the third as a reality that you don't engage in anymore. Your permanent, nonstop experience is that of the fourth. Included in this perpetual arrangement now are my dreams. I dream in fourth-dimensional awareness whenever there are dreams. I react at a dream level with the same awareness as I do awake. My dreams are just as joyful and free as my daily life experience. This is quite a noticeable difference, because I have always been able to remember my dreams and before the shift into the fourth, there were far more unpleasant dreams than uplifting ones. I feel deep gratitude and appreciation for the peace and Satsang that takes place now in my dreams.

Out of Control Thoughts

We have all experienced how crazy our minds are in the third dimension when we sat in meditation, watched our thoughts, and futilely tried to control them. The sages gave the name of "monkey mind" to the antics of a normal three-dimensional mind. More good news! The crazy thoughts of the mind come from the desires of the ego personality. Guess what happens when that ego personality is dissolved and the mind is left behind as you shift into the fourth? That's right! No more out-of-control thoughts or daydreaming. Instead these are replaced by the sweet Presence of Self/Source. I mean a real, tangible, felt Presence that is so comforting that you focus automatically on this instead of the old monkey mind. That's why I shared with you before that all I do during my meditations is purr like a contented cat. Nothing else—just purring. It's so delicious that if my body could take it without cramping, the time I would spend there would be endless.

Another phenomenon worthy of reporting here is the occurrence of practically nonstop inner Satsang going on all the time in the fourth dimension. Once that shift has happened, your own inner fount of wisdom is always bringing you along in this deliverance process. This is very interesting—never the same—never boring. Since we use words to enable us to function in the third, they continue in the fourth, but more of an intuitive nature rather than spoken. Source, Self, Somebody within there is constantly pointing out that what may look like cruel or ruthless behavior is not all that it seems. The inner Satsang flows effortlessly, directly to the point, and always in great humor.

But this is not to say that I walk around with lofty thoughts of God, or virtue, or selfless service to mankind, nor anything even resembling what we might imagine "so-called saints" think about in their spare time. No, there is only a profound gratitude for this new freedom, deep appreciation of natural beauty and art, like classical music, constant, beautiful, and funny Satsang about whatever I happen to be witnessing. There is a nonchalant attitude about life in the fourth with this overwhelming sense of

Presence. I have never laughed so hard or so often in my life as I do now. Everything is so funny! Nothing is too serious or too sacred to giggle about. Now I know that the quintessence of Source for this particular mind/body organism is probably not love or compassion, but an infinite sense of humor that creates, sees, and feels a delicious comedy in all of Its projections. Why else would the ancients have called the workings of Source in appearance as the Leela, or Divine Comedy?

A lot of the time I feel like Alice in Wonderland, walking around a strange new environment, with an inner guide called Satsang pointing out the beauty and humor of every situation. But it's also like walking through a tasteful museum of fine, living art, where at times one is curious and at the same time touched by the beauty and diversity one beholds, but never wanting to change or rearrange a single detail. You get to know on an intuitive level, that it is all perfect just the way it is here and now.

Former Allurements

This part may really scare you if you are still in the third dimension, but I have to be honest and share everything here with you. Once I was shifted into the fourth, I could not think of a single item from the third that still attracted me like it did before. Here's just a partial list: sailboats, airplane, cars, adult toys, all competitive sports, making lots of money, playing at any relationship besides what I refer to as the Sacred Relationship, movies, TV, all books, anything that talks about the story of the 3-D story as though it were real, or any kind of achievement or success. In short, everything that conventional wisdom holds up to those in the third as a worthwhile and worthy goal to strive for has dissolved along with the ego personality.

Perhaps conspicuous by its absence in this list of former allurements is sexual activity. After all, that was one of my driving forces in the third dimension. I maintained a vow of chastity until I was 26 years old because of the priesthood and left the monastery a virgin. In the next 26 years, I did everything possible to make up for all that "lost time." I enjoyed sex so much that it bordered on obsessive-compulsive behavior. Shift happened! Now what?

Well, I am back in the celibacy mode again, this time due to the restrictions of prison life. But sexual enjoyment is definitely still one of my predispositions, so here's what's happening. Among the general population in prison, sex is the number one topic of interest and conversation. The lack of sexual accessibility is the biggest complaint about the system, and it fuels a desire just as burning as the desire for freedom from incarceration. With me, the idea of sex as a desire vanished along with the dissolution of the ego personality, along with all the other desires and preferences. I am now open to enjoy sex again within the closeness of a sacred relationship once I leave this prison/ashram. But it feels about as urgent a priority as getting a haircut, and I am basically bald! So if there was ever a good example of how radical this fourth-dimensional shift really is, I would cite my own freedom from that former 26-year sexual addiction.

But the fourth doesn't leave vacuums as the shift occurs. Instead of all this stuff that is extrinsic to one's Self, my moment-to-moment attraction and complete fullness is felt in the overwhelming sense of Presence. I don't have to reach out for It. It's there for me always and effortlessly. Without even thinking of It, I am filled to overflowing with Its bliss and freedom. You don't have to give up any of your toys from the third. They just vanish into insignificance. And what better way to experience this sense of Presence than just living a simple, ordinary life. Anything to do with fame, success or power, or the norms of conventional wisdom would just distract you from the full enjoyment of this sense of Presence. This is one of those explanations that if you have already shifted, you know what I'm referring to, and if you haven't yet, I feel inadequate trying to fully explain the power of this Presence to fulfill all of oneself. But I can tell you this with confidence and certainty: There is nothing you need, desire, or require from the third that is directly linked to your freedom, joy, or peace in the fourth. It's a self-contained reality that isn't based on the illusion of separation. As you peel away more and more onion layers of old conditioning from the third, your enjoyment of the fourth only increases with familiarity. In the third, familiarity breeds contempt, or at least boredom. But in the fourth, the adventure only increases with the clarity and understanding of deliverance.

Freedom/Limitation Equation

What about that elaborate theory of mine about the Freedom/Limitation balance in every event in life? How does that apply to the fourth? Well, limitation is only possible when there is an ego personality to feel it through resistance. That means this equation is limited to the third dimension only. The fourth is pure and total freedom always. Because dissolution of the ego personality is a prerequisite to the fourth, there's no body home to feel the limitation anymore. There's only one inhabitant of the fourth dimension—Source as Self. No more separation into me and Source. Just I Am That!

Do's and Don'ts For The Fourth Dimension

There aren't any! Do's and don'ts are for religions in the third. They just don't fit in the fourth. For one thing, anyone shifting into the fourth would have a common denominator of *harmlessness*. Once this is established as your *modus operandi*, you can do or not do anything you like. At this point, it's all the same, it's all Source, you can't screw up! Every single individual mind/body organism is unique and has different predispositions, but harmlessness is the underlying common personality trait that transcends all predispositions. It used to be that a sage would break through to the fourth, and soon a following of his students and disciples would want to know how he did it, and how to maintain it. So he would analyze his unique, particular path of destiny and then lay out a big bunch of commandments that ranged from moralistic to dietary regulations. But my experience of the fourth is that it is an energy field of total, absolute freedom in every single area, and that with harmlessness as your only guide, you get to continue your dance, as Source, as a unique one-of-a-kind experience. Spiritual disciplines belong to the third. They are all transcended in the fourth.

As soon as you are shifted, you recognize that others in either the third or the fourth carry their own sacred truth within, which leads to their own sacred actions. You embrace this, and so laying out do's and don'ts for them seems to violate your acceptance of all reality as Source in appearance. You leave behind all questions regarding the third, especially the "WHY?" one. So naturally you have all the answers if you don't have any more questions. I feel strange sometimes during Satsang trying to answer a third-dimension question because my mind doesn't think like that anymore. I left my mind behind in the third, along with my concern for the future, my guilt about the past, and all the fears and addictions that distracted me from the enjoyment of the here and now.

There is another common denominator that comes with the territory that can only be called "detachment" from the results of your actions. It's not something you can work on to acquire either. It just happens naturally with the shift. I can best explain with a recent example. For 17 years now, Pauline and I have owned and operated a resort on the beach in Tulum, Mexico. Over the years, three hurricanes have leveled it, to say nothing of the everyday intrigue and corruption associated with doing business in Mexico. But we love the place. It has always been a high-energy-retreat kind of resort, rather than your typical hotel. Prior to the shift, I had put in over 10 years of hands-on management with this resort, and how well I remember the constant contraction, like a knife in my gut, when dealing with the intrigue there. So when Pauline is up against the wall these days, rebuilding again after Hurricane Roxanne last fall, and still dealing with all those things by herself, she asks me: "How does one maintain a 'nondoing' attitude under these circumstances?" My answer is simple but dangerous. When the shift happens, there is a peace and detachment about the outcome of your actions, no matter what. In the worst-case scenario, you are quite prepared and willing to lose everything, if that is what happens. I can understand her concern at this approach, but once living in the fourth, it doesn't matter anymore whether you win or lose, it's all the same.

Does that mean the 17 years of hard work, a million dollars of repeat construction over the years, and your daughter's future inheritance down the drain don't matter? Yes, strange as it may sound, but true! Your peace, joy, and freedom no longer depend on on any external factors. So I guess this means she won't be asking me to run it any anymore. Actually, operating a business with a sense of total detachment may well be the most efficient way after all. But that world has lost its attraction for me these days, and I doubt if I will return to it.

I can mention here another unique feature of the fourth that might never occur to one before the shift happens. When all resistance is dissolved into what is – as is, and all you are left with is just choiceless awareness, there is a brand new experience of being totally alive in the moment. It's not easy to explain, but I constantly feel so alive and full of awe and wonder at just the very ordinary events of life now. It is the same, ordinary stuff that used to drive me crazy with either boredom or irritation. I am convinced that my former resistance to living life as it happened and never really embracing it moment by moment were the chief obstacles to this new state of throbbing aliveness that hums and glimmers.

Proof of the Fourth Dimension

The most common question I get about this fourth is "But can you prove to me that the fourth is as real as you say it is?" Yes, because I kept asking myself that very same question as the shift occurred. Let's say we were talking about physical growth here. Say that, in my experiments, I grew a foot taller by standing on my head and gargling peanut butter every day for an hour. My proof is a before-and-after photo, so you would probably believe me.

But we are talking about the shift from the third to the fourth dimension here. A little more tricky to prove, no doubt.

All I can tell you is that this shift has occurred for me. It was a happening of Grace and Destiny. It is definitely happening to many others right now. If you knew me before this shift occurred, you might say that my life in the third was the usual balance of freedom and limitation, even though I felt the limitation much more than the freedom. You would also now see an enormous difference in me. I am on fire with joy and freedom. Not just during Satsang, when I can hardly contain my excitement, but continually. The limitation has ended and freedom is my main experience of life now. This would be self-evident if we shared Satsang.

And even more amazing to me is that within my Satsang circles this is also happening to others. Even people I don't know who have read this manuscript before it was published are writing to me about this very same shift happening to them.

What is even more amazing is that they are being knocked over into the fourth dimension with just the touch of a feather compared to the repeated sledge hammer blows of awakening in the past. This is certainly true in my case. The painful death of the ego I described seems to have been replaced by a smoother, quicker transition for those in my Satsang circles, and for those who are in correspondence with me. For many, just reading this journal has been a validation of their own experience, and they have wept tears of joy and recognition. What is encouraging in their shared stories of awakening is that it did not require a crisis as radical or extreme as mine to precipitate their wake-up and shift into the fourth dimension.

I posed a rhetorical question earlier in the book: Are we beginning a new age of freedom that transcends the limitation of the human predicament? It appears we are right on the cutting edge of it. So, like the writers of the New Testament who called their books "the Gospels," which translated means "the Good News," I end this journal by also sharing more good news with you. The New Age of freedom is now drawing near as the fourth dimension. But remember this. It no longer requires doing! Understanding is all there is to it! Enjoy your new freedom!

CHAPTER 42

THE WISDOM OF LAO TZU

Now that I have given away all of my secrets and insights about our journey through this human predicament, maybe you would also like to share some of the Satsang from Lao Tzu and his little book of poetic verses called the *Tao Te Ching*. My vote for the wisest book ever written goes to Lao Tzu for his understanding of what he calls the Tao, and you can just substitute that word for *Source* in this book. Keep in mind that he wrote the *Tao Te Ching* long before Christ, Buddha, or Mohammed ever entered the world of appearance or their words ever became scriptures. Do you see any similarities between our experiences? Here is my interpretation of Lao Tzu's words.

In verse 56, he states that:

> Those who know, won't talk about it.
> Those who talk, don't know about it.

In other words, how do you put into words that which can't be described when you talk about a subject like Source? I don't have any smart answer for you on that but listen to what one of his fans, Po Chui, another poet and an apparent comedian, wrote:

> He who talks, doesn't know.
> He who knows, doesn't talk.
> That is what Lao Tzu told us,
>   in a book of 5000 words.
> If he was the one who knew,
>   how could he have been such a blabbermouth?[1]

My response to that is, all you can do when absorbed by the Presence of Source, is to try and describe how it feels and hope that Grace will bridge the weakness of the words with the understanding beyond those words.

Verse 2
> The sage
>> lives in the world of non-doing.
> He lets things happen
>> but doesn't start them.
> He acts
>> but without presumption.
> He finishes his work
>> but without dwelling on it.

Verse 3
> The sage leads
>> by hollowing their minds
>> but filling their hearts.
> He weakens their ambition
>> and strengthens their resolve.
> He helps
>> people to lose their knowledge
>> and desires.
> He causes
>> confusion in those
>> who think they know.

Verse 5
> The Tao cannot choose sides.
> It is the source of both good and evil.

It sounds to me like he is saying: Consciousness is all there is.

Verse 8
>It is precisely because one is content
>>to simply be
>>>and not compete or compare
>>that there is no fault or blame.

Verse 9
>Chase after gold and security,
>>and you will never be able to protect them.
>If wealth and honor make you arrogant,
>>you will be their prisoner.

Verse 10
>Can you
>>deal with life's vital affairs
>>by simply letting them
>>follow their unfolding?
>In standing back
>>from your own mind
>>you begin to understand all things.

Verse 12
>Thoughts
>>weaken the mind
>Desires
>>weaken the heart.
>Thus the sage
>>can observe the world
>>but trusts his own inner fount of wisdom.

Verses 13 and 14 sum up my wake-up call and the deliverance that followed.

Verse 13
>Simply
>>see the world as yourself.

Embrace
things as they are.

Verse 14
If you know
where you come from,
Then you know
the essence of all wisdom.

Verse 15
If you have
the patience to wait,
gradually the muddy water becomes clear.
If you can
remain in nondoing,
the perfect action
arises by itself.

Verse 16
Creatures come forth in great number,
but each returns to a common source.
Not to know the Source
is to stumble in confusion.

To know the Source
is to be enlightened.

When you know where you come from
you are naturally all-embracing and impartial.
By immersing yourself
in the safety of the Source
you can deal with what life brings to you,
and to the end of your days,
you will suffer no confusion.

Verse 23
>   Devote yourself to the Tao
>   and be one with the Source.
>   Embrace your natural responses
>   and watch everything drop into place.

Verse 28
>   Accept the world as it is.
>   If you do
>   the Tao will be luminous
>   inside you,
>   and you will return
>   to your primal self.

Verse 29
>   For those
>   who would like to improve the world,
>   I see they cannot succeed.
>   For the world
>   is already a sacred vessel,
>   not something that can be acted on.
>   If you try to act on it,
>   you will destroy it.
>   If you try to hold on to it,
>   you will lose it.
>   The sage
>   accepts things exactly as they are.
>   For this reason
>   he avoids extremes, excesses and extravagance.

Verse 30
>   The sage
>   fulfills his purpose in a job and that is all.
>   He understands
>   events are always out of his control,

and attempts to manipulate them
run counter to the Tao.
He achieves his result
but is not proud.
He fulfills his purpose
but is not boastful.
He fulfills his actions
only because he has no other choice.

Verse 35

Whoever is centered in the Tao
can move through life in great safety.
Even in the midst of widespread suffering
the sage sees only
the inscrutable harmony of Source,
and thus feels peace within.

This is the secret of dealing with the pain and suffering
involved in the human predicament.

Verse 37

In the non-doing attitude of the Tao
all things are accomplished.
If rulers could preserve this attitude
all things would transform on their own.
After transformation they would be content
in nameless simplicity and free from desires.
Where there are no desires,
Heaven and Earth will of themselves be right.

Verse 38

The sage
makes no efforts on his own.
He resides in fruitful reality,
and not in blossomy illusion.

Verse 41

When higher men discover the Tao,
    they practice it with diligence.
When average men hear the Tao,
    some things they keep,
    and others they lose.
When inferior men hear the Tao,
    they can only laugh out loud at it.
For if they didn't laugh,
It couldn't be regarded as the Tao.

Verse 42

The average man can't stand to be alone.
But the sage
    utilizes it to embrace his aloneness,
        and to realize
        his Oneness with all that is.

Verse 44

Know contentment with the way things are,
    and you will never be disgraced.
Know satisfaction in what you have,
    and you will long endure.

Verse 48

Those who pursue learning
    daily increase results.
Those who have heard the Tao
    daily drop something.
    (Peeling the onion.)
They decrease until
    they arrive at a point of nondoing.
In doing nothing
    there is nothing left undone.

Verse 52

> Open the doors of the mind to judgments
> Meddle with affairs;
>> your whole life will be troubled.
> Close the doors to desire;
>> your whole life you will not suffer.
> Knowing how to yield in softness is called strength.

Verse 55

> The sage allows everything to come and go
>> without effort or preference.
> Because he has no expectations about results
>> he is never disappointed in how they turn out.

Verse 57

> Gain all of heaven with non-interference.
> Use unconcern with affairs and concepts
>> and watch the world control itself.

Verse 59

> When you have no destination
>> no one knows the end.
> Then you can utilize
>> whatever life brings you.
> This is called,
>> the Way of long life and lasting vision.

Verse 65

> The simplest pattern is the clearest.
>> Content with an ordinary life,
>>> you can show people the way
>> back to their own true nature.

And so with these words of Lao Tzu as a strong validation of a "nondoing" attitude, I can sum up my own understanding of the Tao:

> The Tao is all there is.
> You are not the doer.
> You can embrace whatever is – as is
>   as Source in diversity.
> You might as well just say "YES" to this whole
>   dance of Leela.

[1] Mitchell, S. (Trans.), *Tao Te Ching*. New York: Harper Perennial (1991), *p. 85.*

WAKE UP AND SMELL THE ONIONS

Weekend And Week-long Intensives with Nadeen

Now that you have digested this journal, you may experience a new or renewed yearning for this "new freedom" that the wake-up call provides. When you grasp the direction that this freedom is headed, you know that although it usually occurs in deep stillness, spiritual disciplines do not make it happen. Yet you may be curious about what this shift from seeking to finding and from the third to the fourth dimension is all about.

Reading this book may give you an intellectual understanding of the message, but the Intensives provide much more of an intuitive experience of this shift. They create the "Quickening" energy field that tends to facilitate this process called the "Deliverance." Once you wake up to the realization that Source is all there is, and you are not the doer after all, your own deliverance has begun.

Herein lies an opportunity to join Nadeen in Satsang, exploring the ramifications of this process in your daily life. Together we peel away all those layers of preconditioning that you inherited in the human predicament and regain your original innocence. Then there is nothing left to do but celebrate!

Weekend Intensives are held every other month in the San Francisco Bay area. Other U.S. and Canada Intensive locations may occur by request with a sufficient number of participants.

WEEK-LONG INTENSIVES
IN COSTA RICA

Mile high on a mountain top, overlooking the coffee fields, blue Pacific, and tropical splendor of Costa Rica sits *Pura Vida*, the home and retreat center of Nadeen. Here "seekers" interested in becoming "finders," as well as those who have already shifted, come to sit and play with Nadeen to peel away their onion layers of conditioning in a process that explores the Self-realization of the perfect Pearl of Consciousness that they already possess.

This is a remarkable week of beauty, joy, Satsang, and self-inquiry within the walled Zen gardens and fountains of Pura Vida. Between the morning and evening sessions there is the spa available for yoga, massage, hot tubs, sauna, swimming pool and fitness training. Beyond these walls group hikes explore local rain forests and the rim of an active volcano called Poas. Another excursion will raft the white waters of a nearby river. These Intensives are limited in the number of participants and are held ongoing throughout the year during the first week of every month.

Costa Rica is a peaceful Central American country known for its political stability, democratically elected government and the absence of a national army. One third of its total surface is devoted to National Parks and Natural Reserves. By protecting its natural resources, nature and wildlife, Costa Rica is earning the reputation of being an ecologically conscious country, the *oxygen reserve* of Central America. The weather is consistently perfect at Pura Vida with daytime temperatures of 70° and nighttime lows of 50°.

For full color brochures regarding details of these Intensives and accommodations at Pura Vida, send the attached postcard.